Shakespeare
Explained

The

Sonnets

MARK MUSSARI

INTRODUCTION BY JOSEPH SOBRAN

Special thanks to Nathaniel Strout, professor of English at
Hamilton College in New York, for his expert review of the manuscript.

Other Marshall Cavendish Offices:
Marshall Cavendish International (Asia) Private Limited, 1 New Industrial Road, Singapore 536196 • Marshall
Cavendish International (Thailand) Co Ltd. 253 Asoke, 12th Flr, Sukhumvit 21 Road, Klongtoey Nua, Wattana,
Bangkok 10110, Thailand • Marshall Cavendish (Malaysia) Sdn Bhd, Times Subang, Lot 46, Subang Hi-Tech
Industrial Park, Batu Tiga, 40000 Shah Alam, Selangor Darul Ehsan, Malaysia

Marshall Cavendish is a trademark of Times Publishing Limited
All websites were available and accurate when this book was sent to press.

Library of Congress Cataloguing-in-Publication Data
Mussari, Mark.
The sonnets / by Mark Mussari.
p. cm. — (Shakespeare explained)
Includes bibliographical references and index.
Summary: "A literary analysis of Shakespeare's sonnets. Includes information
on the history and culture of Elizabethan England"—Provided by publisher.
ISBN 978-1-60870-018-9
1. Shakespeare, William, 1564-1616. Sonnets—Juvenile literature.
2. Sonnets, English—History and criticism—Juvenile literature. I. Title.
PR2848.M87 2011
821'.3—dc22
2009041727

Photo research by: Linda Sykes
Getty Images: front cover, 94; Mikhali/Shutterstock: 2–3; Neven Mendrila/Shutterstock: 3; Raciro/istockphoto:
4, 40, 46; Art Parts RF: 6, 8, 13, 26, 27, 34, back cover; ©Nik Wheeler/Corbis: 11; Portraitgalerie, Schloss Ambras,
Innsbruck, Austria/Erich Lessing/Art Resource, NY: 20; Travelshots.com/Alamy: 22; ©Hideo Kurihara/
Alamy: 24; Corbis/Sygma: 29; Andrew Fox/Corbis: 32; Northwind Picture Archive: 39; National Portrait
Gallery, London, UK/The Bridgeman Art Library: 43; By Permission of the Folger Shakespeare Library: 45;
DEA/A. Bergani/De Agostini/Getty Images: 50; Private Collection/Photo ©Rafael Valls Gallery, London, UK/
The Bridgeman Art Library: 59; Tim Graham Photo Library/Getty Images: 63; China Span/Getty Images: 67;
Bridgeman Art Library/Getty Images: 71; Arbury Hall, Warwickshire UK: 79; Victoria and Albert Museum,
London, UK/The Bridgeman Art Library: 89; British Library, London, Great Britain/HIP/Art Resource, NY: 97;
Pinacoteca di Brera, Milan, Italy/Art Resource, NY: 112.

Editor: Megan Comerford
Publisher: Michelle Bisson
Art Director: Anahid Hamparian
Series Design: Kay Petronio

Printed in Malaysia (T)
135642

Contents

Shakespeare and His World

WILLIAM SHAKESPEARE,

OFTEN NICKNAMED "THE BARD," IS, BEYOND ANY COMPARISON, THE MOST TOWERING NAME IN ENGLISH LITERATURE. MANY CONSIDER HIS PLAYS THE GREATEST EVER WRITTEN. HE STANDS OUT EVEN AMONG GENIUSES.

Yet the Bard is also closer to our hearts than lesser writers, and his tremendous reputation should neither intimidate us nor prevent us from enjoying the simple delights he offers in such abundance. It is as if he had written for each of us personally. As he himself put it, "One touch of nature makes the whole world kin."

Such tragedies as *Hamlet*, *Romeo and Juliet*, and *Macbeth* are world famous, still performed onstage and in films. These and other plays have also been adapted for radio, television, opera, ballet, pantomime, novels, comic books, and other media. Two of the best ways to become familiar with them are to watch some of the many fine movies that have been made of them and to listen to recordings of them by some of the world's great actors.

Even Shakespeare's individual characters have lives of their own, like real historical figures. Hamlet is still regarded as the most challenging role ever written for an actor. Roughly as many whole books have been written about Hamlet, an imaginary character, as about actual historical figures such as Abraham Lincoln and Napoleon Bonaparte.

Shakespeare created an amazing variety of vivid characters. One of Shakespeare's most peculiar traits was that he loved his characters so much—even some of his villains and secondary or comic characters—that at times he let them run away with the play, stealing attention from his heroes and heroines.

So in *A Midsummer Night's Dream* audiences remember the absurd and lovable fool Bottom the Weaver better than the lovers who are the main characters. Romeo's friend Mercutio is more fiery and witty than Romeo himself; legend claims that Shakespeare said he had to kill Mercutio or Mercutio would have killed the play.

Shakespeare also wrote dozens of comedies and historical plays, as well as nondramatic poems. Although his tragedies are now regarded as his greatest works, he freely mixed them with comedy and history. And his sonnets are among the supreme love poems in the English language.

It is Shakespeare's mastery of the English language that keeps his words familiar to us today. Every literate person knows dramatic lines such as "Wherefore art thou Romeo?"; "My kingdom for a horse!"; "To be or not to be: that is the question"; "Friends, Romans, countrymen, lend me your ears"; and "What fools these mortals be!" Shakespeare's sonnets are noted for their sweetness: "Shall I compare thee to a summer's day?"

THOU ART ALL MY ART.

SHAKESPEARE'S LANGUAGE

WITHOUT A DOUBT, SHAKESPEARE WAS THE GREATEST MASTER OF THE ENGLISH LANGUAGE WHO EVER LIVED. BUT JUST WHAT DOES THAT MEAN?

Shakespeare's vocabulary was huge, full of references to the Bible as well as Greek and Roman mythology. Yet his most brilliant phrases often combine very simple and familiar words:

"WHAT'S IN A NAME? THAT WHICH WE CALL A ROSE BY ANY OTHER NAME WOULD SMELL AS SWEET."

He has delighted countless millions of readers. And we know him only through his language. He has shaped modern English far more than any other writer.

Or, to put it in more personal terms, you probably quote his words several times every day without realizing it, even if you have never suspected that Shakespeare could be a source of pleasure to you.

So why do so many English-speaking readers find his language so difficult? It is our language, too, but it has changed so much that it is no longer quite the same language—nor a completely different one, either.

Shakespeare's English and ours overlap without being identical. He would have some difficulty understanding us, too! Many of our everyday words and phrases would baffle him.

Shakespeare, for example, would not know what we meant by a *car*, a *radio*, a *movie*, a *television*, a *computer*, or a *sitcom*, since these things did not even exist in his time. Our old-fashioned term *railroad train* would be unimaginable to him, far in the distant future. We would have to explain to him (if we could) what *nuclear weapons, electricity*, and *democracy* are. He would also be a little puzzled by common expressions such as *high-tech, feel the heat, approval ratings, war criminal, judgmental*, and *whoopee cushion*.

So how can we call him "the greatest master of the English language"? It might seem as if he barely spoke English at all! (He would, however, recognize much of our dirty slang, even if he pronounced it slightly differently. His plays also contain many racial insults to Jews, Africans, Italians, Irish, and others. Today he would be called "insensitive.")

Many of the words of Shakespeare's time have become archaic. Words like *thou, thee, thy, thyself*, and *thine*, which were among the most common words in the language in Shakespeare's day, have all but disappeared today. We simply say *you* for both singular and plural, formal and familiar. Most other modern languages have kept their *thou*.

Sometimes the same words now have different meanings. We are apt to be misled by such simple, familiar words as *kind, wonderful, waste, just*, and *dear*, which he often uses in ways that differ from our usage.

Shakespeare also doesn't always use the words we expect to hear, the words that we ourselves would naturally use. When we might automatically say, "I beg your pardon" or just "Sorry," he might say, "I cry you mercy."

Often a glossary and footnotes will solve all three of these problems for us. But it is most important to bear in mind that Shakespeare was often hard for his first audiences to understand. Even in his own time his rich language was challenging. And this was deliberate. Shakespeare was inventing his own kind of English. It remains unique today.

A child doesn't learn to talk by using a dictionary. Children learn first by sheer immersion. We teach babies by pointing at things and saying their names. Yet the toddler always learns faster than we can teach! Even as babies we are geniuses. Dictionaries can help us later, when we already speak and read the language well (and learn more slowly).

So the best way to learn Shakespeare is not to depend on the footnotes and glossary too much, but instead to be like a baby: just get into the flow of the language. Go to performances of the plays or watch movies of them.

THE LANGUAGE HAS A MAGICAL WAY OF TEACHING ITSELF, IF WE LET IT. THERE IS NO REASON TO FEEL STUPID OR FRUSTRATED WHEN IT DOESN'T COME EASILY.

Hundreds of phrases have entered the English language from *Hamlet* alone, including "to hold, as 'twere, the mirror up to nature"; "murder most foul"; "the thousand natural shocks that flesh is heir to"; "flaming youth"; "a countenance more in sorrow than in anger"; "the play's the thing"; "neither a borrower nor a lender be"; "in my mind's eye"; "something is rotten in the state of Denmark"; "alas, poor Yorick"; and "the lady doth protest too much, methinks."

From other plays we get the phrases "star-crossed lovers"; "what's in a name?"; "we have scotched the snake, not killed it"; "one fell swoop"; "it was Greek to me"; "I come to bury Caesar, not to praise him"; and "the most unkindest cut of all"—all these are among our household words. In fact, Shakespeare even gave us the expression "household words." No wonder his contemporaries marveled at his "fine filed phrase" and swooned at the "mellifluous and honey-tongued Shakespeare."

Shakespeare's words seem to combine music, magic, wisdom, and humor:

"THE COURSE OF TRUE LOVE NEVER DID RUN SMOOTH."

"HE JESTS AT SCARS THAT NEVER FELT A WOUND."

"THE FAULT, DEAR BRUTUS, IS NOT IN OUR STARS, BUT IN OURSELVES, THAT WE ARE UNDERLINGS."

"COWARDS DIE MANY TIMES BEFORE THEIR DEATHS; THE VALIANT NEVER TASTE OF DEATH BUT ONCE."

"NOT THAT I LOVED CAESAR LESS, BUT THAT I LOVED ROME MORE."

"THERE ARE MORE THINGS IN HEAVEN AND EARTH, HORATIO, THAN ARE DREAMT OF IN YOUR PHILOSOPHY."

"BREVITY IS THE SOUL OF WIT."

"THERE'S A DIVINITY THAT SHAPES OUR ENDS, ROUGH-HEW THEM HOW WE WILL."

Four centuries after Shakespeare lived, to speak English is to quote him. His huge vocabulary and linguistic fertility are still astonishing. He has had a powerful effect on all of us, whether we realize it or not. We may wonder how it is even possible for a single human being to say so many memorable things.

Only the King James translation of the Bible, perhaps, has had a more profound and pervasive influence on the English language than Shakespeare. And, of course, the Bible was written by many authors over many centuries, and the King James translation, published in 1611, was the combined effort of many scholars.

EARLY LIFE

So who, exactly, was Shakespeare? Mystery surrounds his life, largely because few records were kept during his time. Some people have even doubted his identity, arguing that the real author of Shakespeare's plays must have been a man of superior formal education and wide experience. In a sense such doubts are a natural and understandable reaction to his rare, almost miraculous powers of expression, but some people feel that the doubts themselves show a lack of respect for the supremely human poet.

Most scholars agree that Shakespeare was born in the town of Stratford-upon-Avon in the county of Warwickshire, England, in April 1564. He was baptized, according to local church records, Gulielmus (William) Shakspere (the name was spelled in several different ways) on April 26 of that year. He was one of several children, most of whom died young.

His father, John Shakespeare (or Shakspere), was a glove maker and, at times, a town official. He was often in debt or being fined for unknown delinquencies, perhaps failure to attend church regularly. It is suspected that John was a recusant (secret and illegal) Catholic, but there is no proof. Many

SHAKESPEARE'S CHILDHOOD HOME IS CARED FOR BY AN INDEPENDENT CHARITY, THE SHAKESPEARE BIRTHPLACE TRUST, IN STRATFORD-UPON-AVON, WARWICKSHIRE, ENGLAND.

scholars have found Catholic tendencies in Shakespeare's plays, but whether Shakespeare was Catholic or not we can only guess.

At the time of Shakespeare's birth, England was torn by religious controversy and persecution. The country had left the Roman Catholic Church during the reign of King Henry VIII, who had died in 1547. Two of Henry's children, Edward and Mary, ruled after his death. When his daughter Elizabeth I became queen in 1558, she upheld his claim that the monarch of England was also head of the English Church.

Did William attend the local grammar school? He was probably entitled to, given his father's prominence in Stratford, but again, we face a frustrating absence of proof, and many people of the time learned to read very well without schooling. If he went to the town school, he would also have learned the rudiments of Latin.

We know very little about the first half of William's life. In 1582, when he was eighteen, he married Anne Hathaway, eight years his senior. Their first daughter, Susanna, was born six months later. The following year they had twins, Hamnet and Judith.

At this point William disappears from the records again. By the early 1590s we find "William Shakespeare" in London, a member of the city's leading acting company, called the Lord Chamberlain's Men. Many of Shakespeare's greatest roles, we are told, were first performed by the company's star, Richard Burbage.

Curiously, the first work published under (and identified with) Shakespeare's name was not a play but a long erotic poem, *Venus and Adonis*, in 1593. It was dedicated to the young Earl of Southampton, Henry Wriothesley.

Venus and Adonis was a spectacular success, and Shakespeare was immediately hailed as a major poet. In 1594 he dedicated a longer, more serious poem to Southampton, *The Rape of Lucrece*. It was another hit, and for many years, these two poems were considered Shakespeare's greatest works, despite the popularity of his plays.

"MINE EYE AND HEART ARE AT MORTAL WAR."

SHAKESPEARE EXPLAINED: THE SONNETS

SHAKESPEARE ON FILM: A SAMPLER

TODAY MOVIES, NOT LIVE PLAYS, ARE THE MORE POPULAR ART FORM. FORTUNATELY MOST OF SHAKESPEARE'S PLAYS HAVE BEEN FILMED, AND THE BEST OF THESE MOVIES OFFER AN EXCELLENT WAY TO MAKE THE BARD'S ACQUAINTANCE. RECENTLY, KENNETH BRANAGH HAS BECOME A RESPECTED CONVERTER OF SHAKESPEARE'S PLAYS INTO FILM.

As You Like It

One of the earliest screen versions of *As You Like It* is the 1936 film starring Laurence Olivier as Orlando and Elisabeth Bergner as Rosalind. The *New York Times*, in a movie review, praised both the directorial interpretation and the actors' portrayals. British actress Helen Mirren starred in a 1978 BBC production that was filmed entirely outdoors. The most recent film version, directed by renowned Shakespearean actor Kenneth Branagh, aired in 2006 on HBO. Set in nineteenth-century Japan, it is visually stunning and a decent interpretation of the play. It also boasts an impressive supporting cast, including Kevin Kline as Jaques, Alfred Molina as Touchstone, and Romola Garai as Celia.

Hamlet

Hamlet, Shakespeare's most famous play, has been well filmed several times. In 1948 Laurence Olivier won three Academy

Awards—for best picture, best actor, and best director—for his version of the play. The film allowed him to show some of the magnetism that made him famous on the stage. Nobody spoke Shakespeare's lines more thrillingly.

The young Derek Jacobi played Hamlet in a 1980 BBC production of the play, with Patrick Stewart (now best known for *Star Trek: The Next Generation*) as the guilty king. Jacobi, like Olivier, has a gift for speaking the lines freshly; he never seems to be merely reciting the famous and familiar words. But whereas Olivier has animal passion, Jacobi is more intellectual. It is fascinating to compare the ways these two outstanding actors play Shakespeare's most complex character.

Franco Zeffirelli's 1990 *Hamlet*, starring Mel Gibson, is fascinating in a different way. Gibson, of course, is best known as an action hero, and he is not well suited to this supremely witty and introspective role, but Zeffirelli cuts the text drastically, and the result turns *Hamlet* into something that few people would have expected: a short, swiftly moving action movie. Several of the other characters are brilliantly played.

Henry IV, Part One

The 1979 BBC Shakespeare series production does a commendable job in this straightforward approach to the play. Battle scenes are effective despite obvious restrictions in an indoor studio setting. Anthony Quayle gives jovial Falstaff a darker edge, and Tim Pigott-Smith's Hotspur is buoyed by some humor. Jon Finch plays King Henry IV with noble authority, and David Gwillim gives Hal a surprisingly successful transformation from boy prince to heir apparent.

Julius Caesar

No really good movie of *Julius Caesar* exists, but the 1953 film, with Marlon Brando as Mark Antony, will do. James Mason is a thoughtful Brutus, and John Gielgud, then ranked with Laurence Olivier among the greatest Shakespearean actors, plays the villainous Cassius. The film is rather dull, and Brando is out of place in a Roman toga, but it is still worth viewing.

King Lear

In the past century, *King Lear* has been adapted for film approximately fifteen times. Peter Brook directed a bleak 1971 version starring British actor Paul Scofield as Lear. One of the best film versions of *King Lear*, not surprisingly, features Laurence Olivier in the title role. The 1983 British TV version, directed by Michael Elliott, provides a straightforward interpretation of the play, though the visual quality may seem dated to the twenty-first–century viewer. Olivier won an Emmy for Outstanding Lead Actor for his role.

Macbeth

Roman Polanski is best known as a director of thrillers and horror films, so it may seem natural that he should have done his 1971 *The Tragedy of Macbeth* as an often-gruesome slasher flick. But this is also one of the most vigorous of all Shakespeare films. Macbeth and his wife are played by Jon Finch and Francesca Annis, neither known for playing Shakespeare, but they are young and attractive in roles that are usually given to older actors, which gives the story a fresh flavor.

The Merchant of Venice

Once again the matchless Sir Laurence Olivier delivers a great performance as Shylock with his wife Joan Plowright as Portia in the 1974 TV film, adapted from the 1970 National Theater (of Britain) production. A 1980 BBC offering features Warren Mitchell as Shylock and Gemma Jones as Portia, with John Rhys-Davies as Salerio. The most recent production, starring Al Pacino as Shylock, Jeremy Irons as Antonio, and Joseph Fiennes as Bassanio, was filmed in Venice and released in 2004.

A Midsummer Night's Dream

Because of the prestige of his tragedies, we tend to forget how many comedies Shakespeare wrote—nearly twice the number of tragedies. Of these perhaps the most popular has always been the enchanting, atmospheric, and very silly masterpiece *A Midsummer Night's Dream*.

In more recent times several films have been made of *A Midsummer Night's Dream*. Among the more notable have been Max Reinhardt's 1935 black-and-white version, with Mickey Rooney (then a child star) as Puck.

Of the several film versions, the one starring Kevin Kline as Bottom and Stanley Tucci as Puck, made in 1999 with nineteenth-century costumes and directed by Michael Hoffman, ranks among the finest, and is surely one of the most sumptuous to watch.

Othello

Orson Welles did a budget European version in 1952, now available as a restored DVD. Laurence Olivier's 1965 film performance is predictably remarkable, though it has been said that he would only approach the part by honoring, even emulating, Paul Robeson's definitive interpretation that ran on Broadway in 1943. (Robeson was the first black actor to play Othello, the Moor of Venice, and he did so to critical acclaim, though sadly his performance was never filmed.) Maggie Smith plays a formidable Desdemona opposite Olivier, and her youth and energy will surprise younger audiences who know her only from the *Harry Potter* films. Laurence Fishburne brilliantly portrayed Othello in the 1995 film, costarring with Kenneth Branagh as a surprisingly human Iago, though Irène Jacob's Desdemona was disappointingly weak.

Richard III

Many well-known actors have portrayed the villainous Richard III on film. Of course, Laurence Olivier stepped in to play the role of Richard in a 1955 version he also directed. Director Richard Loncraine chose to set his 1995 film version in Nazi Germany. The movie, which starred Ian McKellen as Richard, was nominated for two Oscars; McKellen was nominated for a Golden Globe for his performance. The World War II interpretation also featured Robert Downey Jr. as Rivers, Kristin Scott Thomas as Lady Anne, and Maggie Smith (from the *Harry Potter* movies) as the Duchess of York. A 2008 version, directed by and starring Scott Anderson, is set in modern-day Los Angeles. Prolific actor David Carradine portrays Buckingham.

Romeo and Juliet

This, the world's most famous love story, has been filmed many times, twice very successfully over the last generation. Franco Zeffirelli directed a hit version in 1968 with Leonard Whiting and the rapturously pretty Olivia Hussey, set in Renaissance Italy. Baz

Luhrmann made a much more contemporary version, with a loud rock score, starring Leonardo DiCaprio and Claire Danes, in 1996.

It seems safe to say that Shakespeare would have preferred Zeffirelli's movie, with its superior acting and rich, romantic, sun-drenched Italian scenery.

The Taming of the Shrew

Franco Zeffirelli's 1967 film version of *The Taming of the Shrew* starred Elizabeth Taylor as Kate and Richard Burton as Petruchio. Shakespeare's original lines were significantly cut and altered to accommodate both the film media and Taylor's inexperience as a Shakespearean actress.

Gil Junger's 1999 movie *10 Things I Hate About You* is loosely based on Shakespeare's play. Julia Stiles and Heath Ledger star in this interpretation set in a modern-day high school. In 2005 BBC aired a version of Shakespeare's play set in twenty-first-century England. Kate is a successful, driven politician who succumbs to cash-strapped Petruchio, played by Rufus Sewell.

The Tempest

A 1960 Hallmark Hall of Fame production featured Maurice Evans as Prospero, Lee Remick as Miranda, Roddy McDowall as Ariel, and Richard Burton as Caliban. The special effects are primitive and the costumes are ludicrous, but it moves along at a fast pace. Another TV version aired in 1998 and was nominated for a Golden Globe. Peter Fonda played Gideon Prosper, and Katherine Heigl played his daughter Miranda Prosper. Sci-fi fans may already know that the classic 1956 film *Forbidden Planet* is modeled on themes and characters from the play.

Twelfth Night

Trevor Nunn adapted the play for the 1996 film he also directed in a rapturous Edwardian setting, with big names like Helena Bonham Carter, Richard E. Grant, Imogen Stubbs, and Ben Kingsley as Feste. A 2003 film set in modern Britain provides an interesting multicultural experience; it features an Anglo-Indian cast with Parminder Nagra (*Bend It Like Beckham*) playing Viola. For the truly intrepid, a twelve-minute silent film made in 1910 does a fine job of capturing the play through visual gags and over-the-top gesturing.

THESE FILMS HAVE BEEN SELECTED FOR SEVERAL QUALITIES: APPEAL AND ACCESSIBILITY TO MODERN AUDIENCES, EXCELLENCE IN ACTING, PACING, VISUAL BEAUTY, AND, OF COURSE, FIDELITY TO SHAKESPEARE. THEY ARE THE MOTION PICTURES WE JUDGE MOST LIKELY TO HELP STUDENTS UNDERSTAND THE SOURCE OF THE BARD'S LASTING POWER.

SHAKESPEARE'S THEATER

Today we sometimes speak of "live entertainment." In Shakespeare's day, of course, all entertainment was live, because recordings, films, television, and radio did not yet exist. Even printed books were a novelty.

In fact, most communication in those days was difficult. Transportation was not only difficult but slow, chiefly by horse and boat. Most people were illiterate peasants who lived on farms that they seldom left; cities grew up along waterways and were subject to frequent plagues that could wipe out much of the population within weeks.

Money—in coin form, not paper—was scarce and hardly existed outside the cities. By today's standards, even the rich were poor. Life was precarious. Most children died young, and famine or disease might kill anyone at any time. Everyone was familiar with death. Starvation was not rare or remote, as it is to most of us today. Medical care was poor and might kill as many people as it healed.

ELIZABETH I, A GREAT PATRON OF POETRY AND THE THEATER, WROTE SONNETS AND TRANSLATED CLASSIC WORKS.

This was the grim background of Shakespeare's theater during the reign of Queen Elizabeth I, who ruled from 1558 until her death in 1603. During that period England was also torn by religious conflict, often violent, among Roman Catholics who were loyal to the pope, adherents of the Church of England who were loyal to the queen, and the Puritans who would take over the country in the revolution of 1642.

Under these conditions, most forms of entertainment were luxuries that were out of most people's reach. The only way to hear music was to be in the actual physical presence of singers or musicians with their instruments, which were primitive by our standards.

One brutal form of entertainment, popular in London, was bearbaiting. A bear was blinded and chained to a stake, where fierce dogs called mastiffs were turned loose to tear him apart. The theaters had to compete with the bear gardens, as they were called, for spectators.

The Puritans, or radical Protestants, objected to bearbaiting and tried to ban it. Despite their modern reputation, the Puritans were anything but conservative. Conservative people, attached to old customs, hated the Puritans. They seemed to upset everything. (Many of America's first settlers, such as the Pilgrims who came over on the *Mayflower*, were dissidents who were fleeing the Church of England.)

Plays were extremely popular, but they were primitive, too. They had to be performed outdoors in the afternoon because of the lack of indoor lighting. Often the "theater" was only an enclosed courtyard. Probably the versions of Shakespeare's plays that we know today were not used in full, but shortened to about two hours for actual performance.

But eventually more regular theaters were built, featuring a raised stage extending into the audience. Poorer spectators (illiterate "groundlings") stood on the ground around it, at times exposed to rain and snow. Wealthier people sat in raised tiers above. Aside from some costumes, there were few props or special effects and almost no scenery. Much had to be imagined: Whole battles might be represented by a few actors with swords. Thunder might be simulated by rattling a sheet of tin offstage.

The plays were far from realistic and, under the conditions of the time, could hardly try to be. Above the rear of the main stage was a small balcony. (It was this balcony from which Juliet spoke to Romeo.) Ghosts and witches might appear by entering through a trapdoor in the stage floor.

Unlike the modern theater, Shakespeare's Globe Theater—he describes it as "this wooden O"—had no curtain separating the stage from the audience. This allowed intimacy between the players and the spectators.

THE RECONSTRUCTED GLOBE THEATER WAS COMPLETED IN 1997 AND IS LOCATED IN LONDON, JUST 200 YARDS (183 METERS) FROM THE SITE OF THE ORIGINAL.

I FAINT WHEN I OF YOU DO WRITE.

The spectators probably reacted rowdily to the play, not listening in reverent silence. After all, they had come to have fun! And few of them were scholars. Again, a play had to amuse people who could not read.

The lines of plays were written and spoken in prose or, more often, in a form of verse called iambic pentameter (ten syllables with five stresses per line). There was no attempt at modern realism. Only males were allowed on the stage, so some of the greatest women's roles ever written had to be played by boys or men. (The same is true, by the way, of the ancient Greek theater.)

Actors had to be versatile, skilled not only in acting, but also in fencing, singing, dancing, and acrobatics. Within its limitations, the theater offered a considerable variety of spectacles.

Plays were big business, not yet regarded as high art, sponsored by important and powerful people (the queen loved them as much as the groundlings did). The London acting companies also toured and performed in the provinces. When plagues struck London, the government might order the theaters to be closed to prevent the spread of disease among crowds. (They remained empty for nearly two years from 1593 to 1594.)

As the theater became more popular, the Puritans grew as hostile to it as they were to bearbaiting. Plays, like books, were censored by the government, and the Puritans fought to increase restrictions, eventually banning any mention of God and other sacred topics on the stage.

In 1642 the Puritans shut down all the theaters in London, and in 1644 they had the Globe demolished. The theaters remained closed until Charles's son, King Charles II, was restored to the throne in 1660 and the hated Puritans were finally vanquished.

But, by then, the tradition of Shakespeare's theater had been fatally interrupted. His plays remained popular, but they were often rewritten by inferior dramatists, and it was many years before they were performed (again) as he had originally written them.

THE ROYAL SHAKESPEARE THEATER, IN STRATFORD-UPON-AVON, WAS CLOSED IN 2007 TO BUILD A 1,000-SEAT AUDITORIUM.

Today, of course, the plays are performed both in theaters and in films, sometimes in costumes of the period (ancient Rome for *Julius Caesar*, medieval England for *Henry V*), sometimes in modern dress (*Richard III* has recently been reset in England in the 1930s).

PLAYS

In the England of Queen Elizabeth I, plays were enjoyed by all classes of people, but they were not yet respected as a serious form of art.

Shakespeare's plays began to appear in print in individual, or quarto, editions in 1594, but none of these bore his name until 1598. Although his tragedies are now ranked as his supreme achievements, his name was first associated with comedies and with plays about English history.

The dates of Shakespeare's plays are notoriously hard to determine. Few performances of them were documented; some were not printed until decades after they first appeared on the stage. Mainstream scholars generally place most of the comedies and histories in the 1590s, admitting that this time frame is no more than a widely accepted estimate.

The three parts of *King Henry VI*, culminating in a fourth part, *Richard III*, deal with the long and complex dynastic struggle or civil wars known as the Wars of the Roses (1455–1487), one of England's most turbulent periods. Today it is not easy to follow the plots of these plays.

It may seem strange to us that a young playwright should have written such demanding works early in his career, but they were evidently very popular with the Elizabethan public. Of the four, only *Richard III*, with its wonderfully villainous starring role, is still often performed.

Even today, one of Shakespeare's early comedies, *The Taming of the Shrew*, remains a crowd-pleaser. (It has enjoyed success in a 1999 film adaptation, *10 Things I Hate About You*, with Heath Ledger and Julia Stiles.) The story is simple: The enterprising Petruchio resolves to marry a rich

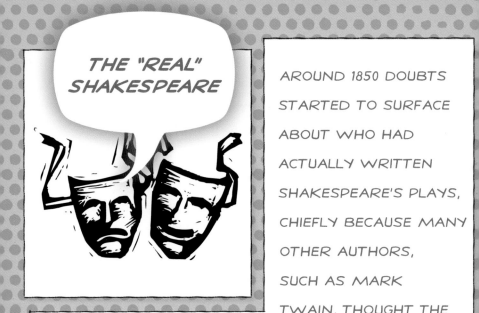

THE "REAL" SHAKESPEARE

AROUND 1850 DOUBTS STARTED TO SURFACE ABOUT WHO HAD ACTUALLY WRITTEN SHAKESPEARE'S PLAYS, CHIEFLY BECAUSE MANY OTHER AUTHORS, SUCH AS MARK TWAIN, THOUGHT THE PLAYS' AUTHOR WAS TOO WELL EDUCATED AND KNOWLEDGEABLE TO HAVE BEEN THE MODESTLY SCHOOLED MAN FROM STRATFORD.

Who, then, was the real author? Many answers have been given, but the three leading candidates are Francis Bacon, Christopher Marlowe, and Edward de Vere, Earl of Oxford.

Francis Bacon (1561-1626)

Bacon was a distinguished lawyer, scientist, philosopher, and essayist. Many considered him one of the great geniuses of his time, capable of any literary achievement, though he wrote little poetry and, as far as we know, no dramas. When people began to suspect that "Shakespeare" was only a pen name, he seemed like a natural candidate. But his writing style was vastly different from the style of the plays.

Christopher Marlowe (1564-1593)

Marlowe wrote several excellent tragedies in a style much like that of the Shakespeare tragedies, though without the comic blend. But he was reportedly killed in a mysterious incident in 1593, before most of the Bard's plays existed. Could his death have been faked? Is it possible that he lived on for decades in hiding, writing under a pen name? This is what his advocates contend.

Edward de Vere, Earl of Oxford (1550-1604)

Oxford is now the most popular and plausible alternative to the lad from Stratford. He had a high reputation as a poet and playwright in his day, but his life was full of scandal. That controversial life seems to match what the poet says about himself in the sonnets, as well as many events in the plays (especially *Hamlet*). However, he died in 1604, and most scholars believe this rules him out as the author of plays that were published after that date.

THE GREAT MAJORITY OF EXPERTS REJECT THESE AND ALL OTHER ALTERNATIVE CANDIDATES, STICKING WITH THE TRADITIONAL VIEW, AFFIRMED IN THE 1623 FIRST FOLIO OF THE PLAYS, THAT THE AUTHOR WAS THE MAN FROM STRATFORD. THAT REMAINS THE SAFEST POSITION TO TAKE, UNLESS STARTLING NEW EVIDENCE TURNS UP, WHICH, AT THIS LATE DATE, SEEMS HIGHLY UNLIKELY.

young woman, Katherina Minola, for her wealth, despite her reputation for having a bad temper. Nothing she does can discourage this dauntless suitor, and the play ends with Kate becoming a submissive wife. It is all the funnier for being unbelievable.

With *Romeo and Juliet* the Bard created his first enduring triumph. This tragedy of "star-crossed lovers" from feuding families is known around the world. Even people with only the vaguest knowledge of Shakespeare are often aware of this universally beloved story. It has inspired countless similar stories and adaptations, such as the hit musical *West Side Story*.

By the mid-1590s Shakespeare was successful and prosperous, a partner in the Lord Chamberlain's Men. He was rich enough to buy New Place, one of the largest houses in his hometown of Stratford.

Yet, at the peak of his good fortune came the worst sorrow of his life: Hamnet, his only son, died in August 1596 at the age of eleven, leaving nobody to carry on his family name, which was to die out with his two daughters.

Our only evidence of his son's death is a single line in the parish burial register. As far as we know, this crushing loss left no mark on Shakespeare's work. As far as his creative life shows, it was as if nothing had happened. His silence about his grief may be the greatest puzzle of his mysterious life, although, as we shall see, others remain.

During this period, according to traditional dating (even if it must be somewhat hypothetical), came the torrent of Shakespeare's mightiest works. Among these was another quartet of English history plays, this one centering on the legendary King Henry IV, including *Richard II* and the two parts of *Henry IV*.

Then came a series of wonderful romantic comedies: *Much Ado About Nothing*, *As You Like It*, and *Twelfth Night*.

In 1598 the clergyman Francis Meres, as part of a larger work, hailed

ACTOR JOSEPH FIENNES PORTRAYED THE BARD IN THE 1998 FILM *SHAKESPEARE IN LOVE*, DIRECTED BY JOHN MADDEN.

Shakespeare as the English Ovid, supreme in love poetry as well as drama. "The Muses would speak with Shakespeare's fine filed phrase," Meres wrote, "if they would speak English." He added praise of Shakespeare's "sugared sonnets among his private friends." It is tantalizing; Meres seems to know something of the poet's personal life, but he gives us no hard information. No wonder biographers are frustrated.

Next the Bard returned gloriously to tragedy with *Julius Caesar*. In the play Caesar has returned to Rome in great popularity after his military triumphs. Brutus and several other leading senators, suspecting that Caesar means to make himself king, plot to assassinate him. Midway through the play, after the assassination, comes one of Shakespeare's most famous scenes. Brutus speaks at Caesar's funeral. But then Caesar's friend Mark Antony delivers a powerful attack on the conspirators, inciting the mob to fury. Brutus and the others, forced to flee Rome, die in the ensuing civil war. In the end the spirit of Caesar wins after all. If Shakespeare had written nothing after *Julius Caesar*, he would still have been remembered as one of the greatest playwrights of all time. But his supreme works were still to come.

Only Shakespeare could have surpassed *Julius Caesar*, and he did so with *Hamlet* (usually dated about 1600). King Hamlet of Denmark has died, apparently bitten by a poisonous snake. Claudius, his brother, has married the dead king's widow, Gertrude, and become the new king, to the disgust and horror of Prince Hamlet. The ghost of old Hamlet appears to young Hamlet, reveals that he was actually poisoned by Claudius, and demands revenge. Hamlet accepts this as his duty, but cannot bring himself to kill his hated uncle. What follows is Shakespeare's most brilliant and controversial plot.

The story of *Hamlet* is set against the religious controversies of the Bard's time. Is the ghost in hell or purgatory? Is Hamlet Catholic or Protestant? Can revenge ever be justified? We are never really given the answers to such questions. But the play reverberates with them.

THE KING'S MEN

In 1603 Queen Elizabeth I died, and King James VI of Scotland became King James I of England. He also became the patron of Shakespeare's acting company, so the Lord Chamberlain's Men became the King's Men. From this point on, we know less of Shakespeare's life in London than in Stratford, where he kept acquiring property.

In the later years of the sixteenth century Shakespeare had been a rather elusive figure in London, delinquent in paying taxes. From 1602 to 1604 he lived, according to his own later testimony, with a French immigrant family named Mountjoy. After 1604 there is no record of any London residence for Shakespeare, nor do we have any reliable recollection of him or his whereabouts by others. As always, the documents leave much to be desired.

Nearly as great as *Hamlet* is *Othello*, and many regard *King Lear*, the heartbreaking tragedy about an old king and his three daughters, as Shakespeare's supreme tragedy. Shakespeare's shortest tragedy, *Macbeth*, tells the story of a Scottish lord and his wife who plot to murder the king of Scotland to gain the throne for themselves. *Antony and Cleopatra*, a sequel to *Julius Caesar*, depicts the aging Mark Antony in love with the enchanting queen of Egypt. *Coriolanus*, another Roman tragedy, is the poet's least popular masterpiece.

SONNETS AND THE END

The year 1609 saw the publication of Shakespeare's Sonnets. Of these 154 puzzling love poems, the first 126 are addressed to a handsome young man, unnamed, but widely believed to be the Earl of Southampton; the rest concern a dark woman, also unidentified. These mysteries are still debated by scholars.

Near the end of his career Shakespeare turned to comedy again, but it was a comedy of a new and more serious kind. Magic plays a large role in these late plays. For example, in *The Tempest*, the exiled duke of Milan, Prospero, uses magic to defeat his enemies and bring about a final reconciliation.

According to the most commonly accepted view, Shakespeare, not yet fifty, retired to Stratford around 1610. He died prosperous in 1616 and left a will that divided his goods, with a famous provision leaving his wife "my second-best bed." He was buried in the chancel of the parish church, under a tombstone bearing a crude rhyme:

> GOOD FRIEND, FOR JESUS SAKE FORBEARE,
> TO DIG THE DUST ENCLOSED HERE.
> BLEST BE THE MAN THAT SPARES THESE STONES,
> AND CURSED BE HE THAT MOVES MY BONES.

This epitaph is another hotly debated mystery: did the great poet actually compose these lines himself?

SHAKESPEARE'S GRAVE IN HOLY TRINITY CHURCH, STRATFORD-UPON-AVON. HIS WIFE, ANNE HATHAWAY, IS BURIED BESIDE HIM.

SHAKESPEARE EXPLAINED: THE SONNETS

THE FOLIO

In 1623 Shakespeare's colleagues of the King's Men produced a large volume of the plays (excluding the sonnets and other poems) titled *Mr. William Shakespeare's Comedies, Histories, & Tragedies* with a woodcut portrait of the Bard. As a literary monument it is priceless, containing our only texts of half the plays; as a source of biographical information it is severely disappointing, giving not even the dates of Shakespeare's birth and death.

Ben Jonson, then England's poet laureate, supplied a long prefatory poem saluting Shakespeare as the equal of the great classical Greek tragedians Aeschylus, Sophocles, and Euripides, adding that "He was not of an age, but for all time."

Some would later denigrate Shakespeare. His reputation took more than a century to conquer Europe, where many regarded him as semi-barbarous. His works were not translated before 1740. Jonson himself, despite his personal affection, would deprecate "idolatry" of the Bard. For a time Jonson himself was considered more "correct" than Shakespeare, and possibly the superior artist.

But Jonson's generous verdict is now the whole world's. Shakespeare was not merely of his own age, "but for all time."

"ALL DAYS ARE NIGHTS TO SEE TILL I SEE THEE."

allegory—a story in which characters and events stand for general moral truths. Shakespeare never uses this form simply, but his plays are full of allegorical elements.

alliteration—repetition of one or more initial sounds, especially consonants, as in the saying "through thick and thin," or in Julius Caesar's statement, "veni, vidi, vici."

allusion—a reference, especially when the subject referred to is not actually named, but is unmistakably hinted at.

aside—a short speech in which a character speaks to the audience, unheard by other characters on the stage.

comedy—a story written to amuse, using devices such as witty dialogue (high comedy) or silly physical movement (low comedy). Most of Shakespeare's comedies were romantic comedies, incorporating lovers who endure separations, misunderstandings, and other obstacles but who are finally united in a happy resolution.

deus ex machina—an unexpected, artificial resolution to a play's convoluted plot. Literally, "god out of a machine."

dialogue—speech that takes place among two or more characters.

diction—choice of words for a given tone. A speech's diction may be dignified (as when a king formally addresses his court), comic (as when the ignorant grave diggers debate whether Ophelia deserves a religious funeral), vulgar, romantic, or whatever the dramatic occasion requires. Shakespeare was a master of diction.

Elizabethan—having to do with the reign of Queen Elizabeth I, from 1558 until her death in 1603. This is considered the most famous period in the history of England, chiefly because of Shakespeare and other noted authors (among them Sir Philip Sidney, Edmund Spenser, and Christopher Marlowe). It was also an era of military glory, especially the defeat of the huge Spanish Armada in 1588.

Globe—the Globe Theater housed Shakespeare's acting company, the Lord Chamberlain's Men (later known as the King's Men). Built in 1598, it caught fire and burned down during a performance of *Henry VIII* in 1613.

hyperbole—an excessively elaborate exaggeration used to create special emphasis or a comic effect, as in Montague's remark that his son Romeo's sighs are "adding to clouds more clouds" in *Romeo and Juliet.*

irony—a discrepancy between what a character says and what he or she truly believes, what is expected to happen and what really happens, or what a character says and what others understand.

metaphor—a figure of speech in which one thing is identified with another, such as when Hamlet calls his father a "fair mountain." (See also **simile**.)

monologue—a speech delivered by a single character.

motif—a recurrent theme or image, such as disease in *Hamlet* or moonlight in *A Midsummer Night's Dream*.

oxymoron—a phrase that combines two contradictory terms, as in the phrase "sounds of silence" or Hamlet's remark, "I must be cruel only to be kind."

personification—imparting personality to something impersonal ("the sky wept"); giving human qualities to an idea or an inanimate object, as in the saying "love is blind."

pun—a playful treatment of words that sound alike, or are exactly the same, but have different meanings. In *Romeo and Juliet* Mercutio says, after being fatally wounded, "Ask for me tomorrow and you shall find me a grave man." *Grave* could mean either "a place of burial" or "serious."

simile—a figure of speech in which one thing is compared to another, usually using the word *like* or *as*. (See also **metaphor**.)

soliloquy—a speech delivered by a single character, addressed to the audience. The most famous are those of Hamlet, but Shakespeare uses this device frequently to tell us his characters' inner thoughts.

symbol—a visible thing that stands for an invisible quality, as poison in *Hamlet* stands for evil and treachery.

syntax—sentence structure or grammar. Shakespeare displays amazing variety of syntax, from the sweet simplicity of his songs to the clotted fury of his great tragic heroes, who can be very difficult to understand at a first hearing. These effects are deliberate; if we are confused, it is because Shakespeare means to confuse us.

theme—the abstract subject or message of a work of art, such as revenge in *Hamlet* or overweening ambition in *Macbeth*.

tone—the style or approach of a work of art. The tone of *A Midsummer Night's Dream*, set by the lovers, Bottom's crew, and the fairies, is light and sweet. The tone of *Macbeth*, set by the witches, is dark and sinister.

tragedy—a story that traces a character's fall from power, sanity, or privilege. Shakespeare's well-known tragedies include *Hamlet, Macbeth,* and *Othello.*

tragicomedy—a story that combines elements of both tragedy and comedy, moving a heavy plot through twists and turns to a happy ending.

verisimilitude—having the appearance of being real or true.

understatement—a statement expressing less than intended, often with an ironic or comic intention; the opposite of hyperbole.

SHAKESPEARE AND
HIS SONNETS

The earliest edition of ▶
Shakespeare's sonnets was
printed in 1609. It is unclear
whether or not Shakespeare
authorized the publication.

SHAKE-SPEARES

SONNETS.

Neuer before Imprinted.

AT LONDON
By *G.* Eld for *T. T.*
to be folde by *Iohn Wright,* dw
at Chrift Church gate.
1 6 0 9.

66929 66929

Chapter One

Shakespeare and His Sonnets

DURING THE RENAISSANCE, THE SONNET—A POEM OF FOURTEEN LINES WITH A FIXED PATTERN OF METER AND RHYME—BECAME A POPULAR LITERARY FORM AMONG MANY POETS. THE SONNET FIRST APPEARED IN ITALY IN THE 1200S AND WAS MASTERED BY TWO OF THE BEST-KNOWN ITALIAN POETS: DANTE AND PETRARCH. PETRARCH, WHO WROTE MORE THAN THREE HUNDRED SONNETS EXPRESSING HIS UNFULFILLED LOVE FOR A BEAUTIFUL WOMAN NAMED LAURA, PERFECTED THE SONNET AS A LOVE POEM. THE SONNET ARRIVED IN ENGLAND IN THE EARLY 1500S. AFTER A PERIOD OF EXPERIMENTATION, THE FORM BECAME QUITE FASHIONABLE DURING THE 1590S, SHAKESPEARE'S GREATEST TIME OF PRODUCTION AS A WRITER OF NONDRAMATIC POETRY.

In the original Italian version, the fourteen-line sonnet consisted of two parts: an octave of eight lines with a specific rhyme scheme and a sestet of six more lines with its own rhyme scheme. The British poet Thomas Wyatt created a uniquely English form by separating the sestet's last two lines into a rhyming couplet. Wyatt's friend Henry Howard, the Earl of Surrey, made an even bolder change: he altered the rhyme scheme so that the poem consisted of three groups of four lines called quatrains—each with its own rhyme scheme—along with the closing couplet.

The Elizabethan, or Shakespearean, sonnet, as the English form came to be known, usually followed one of two rhyme schemes: *abba cddc effe gg* or *abab cdcd efef gg*. All but two of Shakespeare's sonnets followed the latter rhyme scheme. Within the specific framework of each sonnet, Shakespeare develops his thoughts and often his images step-by-step throughout the three quatrains. He summarizes or comments on his thoughts in the closing couplet.

During Shakespeare's time, a number of English poets created sequences, or groups, of sonnets in the style of Petrarch. The sonnets in a sequence often all comment on some aspect of a relationship. For example, Sir Philip Sidney wrote all of his sonnets in honor of an unrequited love named Stella. A beautiful—usually blond, or "fair"—woman who was unobtainable became the frequent subject of many sonnets and sonnet sequences. Most scholars view Shakespeare's sonnets as a sequence—but one with intriguing twists. The Bard addressed the first 126 to a young man of noble birth, often referred to as the Fair Youth. Sonnets 127 to 152 tell of the speaker's affair with a married woman known only as the Dark Lady. The final two sonnets, 153 and 154, offer commentaries on love.

As Shakespeare's sonnets progress, the Dark Lady also has an affair with the same young man who is the object of the first 126 sonnets. In addition, sonnets 78 to 86 reveal that the Fair Youth has received poems praising him from a rival poet. Therefore, the speaker has been betrayed by both his beloved young friend and his beguiling mistress. However, some scholars question whether Shakespeare really did address them to only two people—or to people who actually existed.

Modern readers must keep in mind that it was not unusual in Shakespeare's time for a man to write poems to his male friends. Today's readers might assume that the impassioned feelings for another man indicate that he must have been homosexual—or at least bisexual. Actually, a number of the sonnets indicate directly that the speaker's feelings for the young man are not sexual. It might be more enlightening to consider that Shakespeare has crafted sonnets about two figures that are quite unlike the unattainable object of female perfection typical of most sonnet sequences.

Scholars do not know the exact dates that Shakespeare composed the sonnets. Their first mention appears in 1598, in a list of contemporary authors compiled by the Elizabethan scholar Francis Meres in his *Palladis Tamia* (a comparative study of English, Greek, Latin, and Italian poets). In 1599, two of the sonnets appeared in an unauthorized "bootleg" edition of love poems called *The Passionate Pilgrim*, collected by William Jaggard, a London bookseller and printer.

Shakespeare's 154 sonnets first appeared in one volume in 1609 under the title *Shake-speares Sonnets. Never before Imprinted*, printed by publisher Thomas Thorpe. Some scholars question the order of the sonnets: the order is Thorpe's, and we have no indication that Shakespeare authorized this edition. Also, some scholars believe the last two sonnets, 153 and 154, were not written by Shakespeare.

Thorpe's 1609 edition includes a dedication: "To the only begetter of these ensuing sonnets Mr. W.H." For centuries scholars have speculated on the identity of "W.H." and whether the initials refer to the young man in the sonnets. Many critics have assumed that the "W.H." of the dedication refers to William Herbert, the Earl of Pembroke. Other scholars believe that the letters *W.H.* are intentionally inverted and refer to Henry Wriothesley, the Earl of Southampton, to whom Shakespeare dedicated two narrative poems. It was not unusual for poets in Shakespeare's time to write works in honor of the patrons who financially supported them.

Still, the reader must remember that the sonnets are artistic creations. There may have been no actual Fair Youth and no Dark Lady in Shakespeare's life. They—and all the situations presented in the sonnets—may simply be creations of his imagination. The Romantic poet William Wordsworth once commented about the sonnets: "With this key Shakespeare unlocked his heart." Although the sonnets may not reflect the Bard's actual feelings, many of the observations and emotions expressed in them are as relevant today as they were four hundred years ago.

HENRY WRIOTHESLEY, THIRD EARL OF SOUTHAMPTON, WAS A WEALTHY PATRON OF SHAKESPEARE.

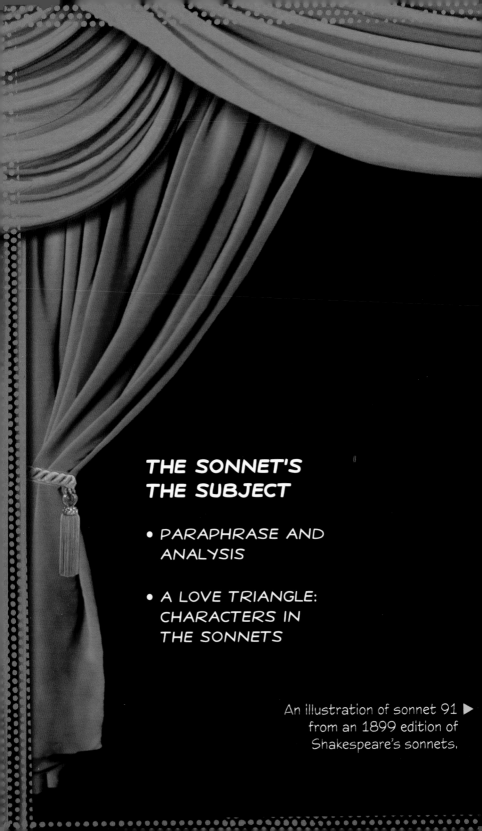

THE SONNET'S THE SUBJECT

- PARAPHRASE AND ANALYSIS

- A LOVE TRIANGLE: CHARACTERS IN THE SONNETS

An illustration of sonnet 91 ▶ from an 1899 edition of Shakespeare's sonnets.

Chapter
Two

CHAPTER TWO

The Sonnet's the Subject

SONNET 2

When forty winters shall besiege thy brow
And dig deep trenches in thy beauty's field,
Thy youth's proud livery, so gazed on now,
Will be a tottered weed of small worth held: 4
Then being asked where all thy beauty lies,
Where all the treasure of thy lusty days,
To say within thine own deep-sunken eyes
Were an all-eating shame, and thriftless praise.   8
How much more praise deserved thy beauty's use,
If thou couldst answer, 'This fair child of mine
Shall sum my count, and make my old excuse,'
Proving his beauty by succession thine.   12
      This were to be new made when thou art old,
      And see thy blood warm when thou feel'st it cold.

This sonnet, like the first seventeen, focuses on one of Shakespeare's favorite subjects: the passing of time. In its development of the speaker's thoughts on this topic, sonnet 2 follows the Shakespearean structure of presenting three examples of one idea in the three quatrains and then summing up these thoughts in the final couplet. As he does in most of the sonnets, Shakespeare develops these observations through various images that illustrate his central argument: time should not be wasted.

In the first quatrain the speaker suggests to his young friend that he should make the most of his life, because youth and beauty will not last forever. The speaker uses "forty winters" to indicate that when the young man turns forty, his looks—like a field that has been dug up and attacked ("besiege") for many years—will diminish.

In the second quatrain the speaker turns to the topic of fading beauty. Since the world will no longer value the young man for his "beauty," he will have used up all the "treasure" of his "lusty" youthful days. In other words, he will no longer be young or physically beautiful. The speaker suggests that, at that point, for the young man to simply say that his beauty lies behind his aged face would be unprofitable ("thriftless"). No one will believe him or care.

Instead, in the final quatrain the speaker suggests that the Fair Youth might receive more "praise" if he could present a child to the world. A beautiful child, the speaker claims, would even the score for growing old. The child's beauty would become a reflection of the young friend's lost fairness, still evident in "succession"—in an heir to his own youth and beauty. The speaker closes by stating that a child would make old beauty "new" and would also make the friend's aged and "cold" blood seem warm.

ANALYSIS

Through the voice of the sonnet's speaker, Shakespeare has created a character who struggles to appear selfless. Particularly in the first seventeen sonnets, the speaker argues repeatedly for what is best for his beloved young friend, often at the speaker's own emotional expense. This selflessness lends a kind of sadness to many of the first 126 sonnets. A reflection of this melancholic emotion expressed in the sonnets is evident in the relationship between the older Antonio and the younger Bassanio in Shakespeare's play *The Merchant of Venice*.

Sonnet 2 offers a prime example of the speaker's selfless nature: he focuses solely on what is good for the young man rather than what might benefit himself. In this sonnet the speaker argues that the young man must take steps to preserve his youthful good looks by having a child, because his beauty is fleeting and dependent on the views of others. This theme dealing with the mutability of life—the lack of permanence in the passing of time—permeates many of the sonnets. It often seems to reflect the speaker's own sense of aging.

Shakespeare's language in this sonnet has military connotations. The winter is besieging, or attacking, the young man's "field" of beauty and, over forty years, deep trenches are dug. The trenches are a metaphor for the lines and wrinkles that accompany age. The use of the word "livery" conjures up images of uniforms on the battlefield. Yet they too will be reduced to a tattered garment ("a tottered weed") with the passing of time. Shakespeare has extended the metaphor of the field throughout the first quatrain. An aging face is compared to a field that has been dug up: once beautiful and now lined with furrows.

The image of buried treasure, a metaphor for precious youth, drives the second quatrain. As he ages, the young friend's beauty will become hidden, and others will ask where it is buried. The speaker warns his friend that claiming that his former beauty is now hiding behind "deep-sunken eyes" would be shameful and self-defeating. The speaker argues that there is no profit in claiming that something still exists when no evidence of it remains. The treasure of youth will remain hidden in the past.

In the third quatrain the speaker arrives at his central point. The young friend, when he is older, might gain some well-deserved "praise" if he could point to a beautiful child and say that the child makes up for growing old. The child's beauty, coming through the line of "succession" from the father, would prove that the young man's own beauty has not completely vanished: "Proving his beauty by succession thine."

The final couplet, as it often does, sums up the thrust of the rest of the sonnet. It also moves the concern of the sonnet from the social (what others might think) to the personal (what would be beneficial for oneself). Having a male child would be rejuvenating ("to be new made") in old age. The speaker tells the Fair Youth that at least he would have the warmth of his child when his own aging blood turns "cold," and that might make the father's blood seem "warm."

SONNET 18

Shall I compare thee to a summer's day?
Thou art more lovely and more temperate.
Rough winds do shake the darling buds of May,
And summer's lease hath all too short a date.   4
Sometime too hot the eye of heaven shines,
And often is his gold complexion dimmed;
And every fair from fair sometime declines,
By chance, or nature's changing course, untrimmed: 8
But thy eternal summer shall not fade
Nor lose possession of that fair thou ow'st,

SHAKESPEARE'S IMAGERY IN SONNET 18 IS EFFECTIVE BECAUSE AN IDYLLIC SUMMER DAY IS SUCH A WIDELY UNDERSTOOD AND EASILY IMAGINED SCENE.

Nor shall Death brag thou wand'rest in his shade
When in eternal lines to time thou grow'st.   12
　　So long as men can breathe or eyes can see,
　　So long lives this, and this gives life to thee.

PARAPHRASE

Sonnet 18, one of the most famous ever written, also begins with one of Shakespeare's most-often quoted lines: "Shall I compare thee to a summer's day?" The next thirteen lines respond to that self-directed challenge by comparing the shifting quality of nature to the consistent beauty of the young friend, captured permanently in the fourteen lines of the poem. Perhaps this sonnet—still in existence some four hundred years after it was written—offers the best proof of what the speaker is saying.

In the first quatrain the speaker establishes that his young friend is more beautiful and moderate than a summer day. To emphasize this, the speaker depicts nature, even in the beauty of spring and summer, as unreliable and untrustworthy. For example, he points out that May winds can sometimes be "rough" and hard on new flowers ("darling buds") and that the warmth of summer only lasts a few months ("all too short a date"). In the next quatrain the speaker points out that the summer sun ("the eye of heaven") is sometimes too hot. At other times the sun becomes lost behind clouds that dim its "gold complexion." No beauty is permanent—"every fair from fair sometime declines"—either by chance or by the changing course of nature. They all decline from their former state of perfection.

SWEET LOVE, RENEW THY FORCE

The final quatrain assures the young friend that the beauty of his youth (his "eternal summer") will never fade, because it has been memorialized in the "eternal lines" of the sonnet. Nor will he lose his perfection: the "fair" he possesses. Even Death will never own the Fair Youth. He will never wander in the darkness ("shade") of the afterlife if he continues to grow, to exist, within the sonnet's lines. The closing couplet encapsulates the speaker's main thought: as long as people live and can read the lines of this sonnet, the Fair Youth will possess "life."

ANALYSIS

Sonnet 18 offers a fine example of the cleverly argumentative quality many of the sonnets possess. The speaker constructs a comparison and then sets out, using figurative language, to prove the conclusion he establishes in the second line: The young man is more lovely and temperate than a summer day. What follows are examples of how a summer's day can be intemperate and even disappointing—a fleeting thing, unlike a sonnet.

Summer storms can bring rough winds, the speaker argues, and sometimes summer's duration (its "lease") can be too short. The speaker employs a metaphor when he refers to the sun as "the eye of heaven" and then extends the metaphor by referring to heaven's "gold complexion" as "dimmed" because of cloud cover. Another argument follows as the speaker points out that beauty drawn from beauty ("fair from fair") often "declines" in value, thanks to both chance and the course of nature.

The "eternal summer" referred to in line 9 reflects the paradoxical idea of endless youth. How can a season last forever? How can youth go on indefinitely? The speaker answers these questions by assuring the young friend that his youth will never "fade." Captured in the lines of the sonnet, it will maintain its beauty ("that fair," repeating the imagery from line 7).

Shakespeare personifies death in line 11: Death both brags and wanders in "his" darkness. Death may also be viewed as an allegorical representation of an abstract concept. In this instance, the broad concept of death is presented as a person—a figure—moving through the darkness. Because the Fair Youth will always exist in the lines of the poem, he will never fade into the oblivion of death's darkness ("shade"). His youth will be immortalized in the sonnet. As long as people read the poem, it "gives life" to the object of the speaker's affection.

SONNET 27

Weary with toil, I haste me to my bed,
The dear repose for limbs with travel tired,
But then begins a journey in my head
To work my mind when body's work's expired;   4
For then my thoughts, from far where I abide,
Intend a zealous pilgrimage to thee,
And keep my drooping eyelids open wide,
Looking on darkness which the blind do see;   8
Save that my soul's imaginary sight
Presents thy shadow to my sightless view,
Which, like a jewel hung in ghastly night,
Makes black night beauteous and her old face new.   12
    Lo, thus, by day my limbs, by night my mind,
    For thee and for myself no quiet find.

PARAPHRASE

In this sonnet the speaker describes how thoughts of his beloved friend keep him awake at night. No matter how tired he is when he goes to bed, he begins a mental journey to his friend. Staring into the darkness, he cannot help but see the Fair Youth's face, and it makes the darkness beautiful, like a star guiding a traveler. Through all of its elegant language, this sonnet says quite simply that there is no rest for the weary.

The first quatrain describes the speaker going to bed after a long day spent in "toil." In his mind, however, he starts to travel ("journey"), keeping his mind active even after his body has become exhausted. In the second quatrain the speaker explains that his thoughts begin to take a pilgrimage to his beloved friend. Therefore, he cannot sleep and stares into the darkness. The third quatrain describes the image of the Fair Youth's face as a jewel hung in the night sky, turning the darkness into a beautiful sight.

During the day his limbs keep him awake, the speaker says in the couplet, and at night it is his mind. Either way, he can find no peace.

ANALYSIS

The word "travel" in this sonnet is sometimes spelled *travail*. Although these two words have different meanings today—*travail* meaning "strenuous mental or physical labor"—they were interchangeable in Shakespeare's time. The sonnet connects journeying with difficult labor.

When a poet carries a comparison between two ideas consciously and cleverly throughout an entire poem, it is often referred to as a *conceit*. Throughout this sonnet, Shakespeare compares the mind's wandering during insomnia to physical journeys that are tiring. He establishes this comparison in the first quatrain: the speaker's mind starts to work just as his body's work is done. The word "expired" also denotes death, perhaps hinting at the speaker's age and his concerns with dying—issues addressed in many of the sonnets.

In the second quatrain the speaker elaborates on the idea of journeying by comparing his mental restlessness to a "pilgrimage," a word carrying religious connotations. In Shakespeare's time, pilgrimages to holy shrines could take days or weeks. The use of "zealous" in line 6 enhances that religious imagery. Does the speaker worship his young friend? Many of the sonnets seem to suggest that he does.

Lying there and staring into the darkness, the speaker sees only one sight, described in the final quatrain. In his mind's eye—in his imagination—he sees his beloved's "shadow," a word meaning "image" and sometimes used to refer to ghosts. Compare this usage of "shadow" with the word "shade" in sonnet 18.

A simile in line 11 compares the young friend's image to a "jewel hung in ghastly night." Still, the dark, horrible night becomes beautiful ("beauteous") because it is illuminated by the imagined face of the Fair Youth. In the closing couplet, the speaker returns to his original comparison: his limbs find no rest during the day because of his toils, and his mind finds no rest at night because he cannot stop thinking of his friend.

SONNET 29

When in disgrace with Fortune and men's eyes
I all alone beweep my outcast state,
And trouble deaf heaven with my bootless cries,
And look upon myself and curse my fate,   4
Wishing me like to one more rich in hope,
Featured like him, like him with friends possessed,
Desiring this man's art, and that man's scope,
With what I most enjoy contented least;   8
Yet in these thoughts myself almost despising,
Haply I think on thee, and then my state
Like to the lark at break of day arising
From sullen earth sings hymns at heaven's gate;   12
　　For thy sweet love rememb'red such wealth brings
　　That then I scorn to change my state with kings.

OUR MINUTES HASTEN TO THEIR END.

PARAPHRASE

In this sonnet of complaint the speaker compares the disappointments of everyday living to the liberating quality of his love for his young friend. The first quatrain flows into the second in this sonnet without the definite pause of a period or a semicolon between lines 4 and 5. Throughout these eight lines, the speaker describes his discouragement and feelings of self-worthlessness when he falls out of favor with the public. He finds himself alone and feeling like an outcast, and he recalls how pointless it seems to pray for change. Heaven, in this instance, is "deaf." He curses his "fate," echoing his reference to "Fortune" in the first line.

Feeling sorry for himself at these moments, the speaker describes how he wishes he were someone else—someone possessing more hope, or one who is better looking, or one who has more friends. He also wishes he had another's talent ("art") or intellectual power ("scope"), and in despair he finds himself least content with the things that usually make him happy.

A turnaround occurs at the beginning of line 9 with the use of "Yet," lending this poem the feel of an Italian sonnet; in that tradition the poem often featured a break in thought (sometimes called a *caesura*) between lines 8 and 9. When the speaker feels most disgusted with himself, he suddenly thinks of his friend. His once "outcast state," now compared to a lark at dawn, sings "hymns" to the same heaven the speaker cursed as "deaf" in the beginning of the sonnet. In the closing couplet, the speaker replaces the wealth he once envied in others with the treasure of the Fair Youth's "sweet love." Now happy with his lot, he no longer wishes he were someone else—not even a king.

Throughout most of this sonnet, the speaker focuses on himself rather than the Fair Youth. A similar approach occurs in sonnet 30, which is another sonnet of complaint. The reference to "men's eyes" offers an example of *synecdoche,* the use of a part of something to represent the whole. Eyes, in this case, signify the way people look at and evaluate the speaker when he is unpopular.

The use of the word "state" in this sonnet points to the way Shakespeare frequently plays with multiple meanings. "State" might suggest the speaker's state of mind, his social status, or even his estate (or wealth). His fortunes—both financially and socially—are apparently tied to all three.

Fortune is personified as an inconstant woman, a popular portrayal in Renaissance literature and art. It may also be a reference to Fortuna, the ancient Roman goddess of luck and fate who could bring positive or negative fortune into people's lives. Its usage emphasizes the speaker's feelings that fate has been fickle with his success. Heaven is personified as being "deaf" because it is not listening to the speaker's pleas. "Heaven" may also be viewed as an example of *metonymy,* in which something closely related stands for something else. Heaven represents God, who does not seem to be answering, or even listening to, the speaker's prayers.

The speaker is wallowing in self-pity, even admitting that he almost despises himself at these instances. Today one might refer to this laundry list of what the speaker feels is wrong with his life as "whining."

Shakespeare conjures up a beautiful simile in line 11: when the speaker's thoughts turn to his beloved friend, he becomes joyful, like a lark singing at dawn. In this image the bird rises from the earth. The speaker comments that at these happy times the gloomy ("sullen") earth transforms into "heaven's gate." He claims that the Fair Youth brings "wealth" to his life, a reference that contrasts his "disgrace with Fortune" in line 1. The speaker is rich with love—a better kind of fortune than gold—richer in his own way than any king. Happy in his love, he would not change his "state" (with a possible pun on "estate") with royalty.

SONNET 55

Not marble nor the gilded monuments
Of princes shall outlive this pow'rful rhyme,
But you shall shine more bright in these contents
Than unswept stone, besmeared with sluttish time.   4
When wasteful war shall statues overturn,
And broils root out the work of masonry,
Nor Mars his sword nor war's quick fire shall burn
The living record of your memory.   8
'Gainst death and all oblivious enmity
Shall you pace forth; your praise shall still find room
Even in the eyes of all posterity
That wear this world out to the ending doom.   12
    So, till the judgment that yourself arise,
    You live in this, and dwell in lovers' eyes.

PARAPHRASE

In this sonnet, another of the Bard's most famous, Shakespeare composes a variation on the classical idea of the enduring quality of writing—of Art—in the face of time's destructive power.

In the first quatrain the speaker claims that his verse ("rhyme") is so "pow'rful" that even marble and golden monuments in honor of royalty will not outlast it. Instead, he tells his beloved Fair Youth that the young man will continue to "shine" more brightly in the lines of the sonnet than some old, neglected stone that time has forgotten.

MOST SCHOLARS AGREE THAT THE FIRST 126 SONNETS ARE ABOUT A YOUNG MAN, OFTEN REFERRED TO AS THE FAIR YOUTH.

In the second quatrain the speaker employs military imagery to reinforce his point. He says that wars ("broils") might destroy statues and stonework ("work of masonry"); yet neither Mars, the Roman god of war, nor the fires of war could ever burn or destroy the memory of the young friend. That memory lives on in this sonnet.

Death may come to others, the speaker claims in the third quatrain, and there may be a hatred ("enmity") that destroys all else; but the friend will still survive ("pace forth"). Praise for him in the form of the poem will still find its place ("room"), even as generations pass, until the end of time ("the ending doom"). The closing couplet refers to the Christian belief in the final Judgment Day, when the dead shall once again live ("arise"). Until that day, the speaker claims that the young man lives on whenever people—especially lovers—read this sonnet.

ANALYSIS

A number of scholars have pointed out Shakespeare's debt to ancient Roman poets such as Horace and Ovid, both of whom wrote about the immortality of poetry. Unlike his predecessors, however, Shakespeare does not focus his sonnet merely on his own ability to compose lasting lines of poetry. On the surface, at least, he is not writing in praise of himself. Instead, his purpose appears to immortalize his friend: it is the memory of the Fair Youth that will outlast time and destruction. Curiously, the speaker offers us nothing specific about the friend and his worth or why he deserves this lasting paean, a song of praise to his existence. Other poets have written songs of praise to their beloveds but usually praise specific attributes.

As in a number of sonnets, death imagery plays an important role in this one. "Monuments" and "unswept stone" conjure up images of graves and cemeteries. Yet the speaker argues that golden statues honoring the dead are no match for the longevity of poetry. In the "contents" of this sonnet, the Fair Youth will "shine more bright" than any gold statue of some dead prince. The speaker's beloved friend will "pace forth," even past the oblivion—the complete destruction—caused by "enmity" in wars. In "the ending doom" and "the judgment," the speaker alludes to the final day of judgment, when the dead shall be resurrected. The Fair Youth's memory will be preserved until the end of time when everything—when the entire world—is destroyed. Through the poem, his memory will live until he rises again, according to Christian doctrine, with Christ. Death, in sonnet 55, can be overcome.

Time often works in the service of Death in the sonnets. In line 4, the speaker refers to time—the villain in so many of the sonnets—as "sluttish," or dirty, untidy, and grimy. Stones may become dirty and dim over time, but through poetry the Fair Youth "shall shine more bright."

As we have seen previously in sonnets 2 and 18, the correlation between time and death was an important one to Shakespeare. The speaker struggles to find ways for his young friend to overcome time's inevitable cost—death—either through the lines of poetry or the creation of children. Readers might also consider the speaker's own quest for immortality through his art.

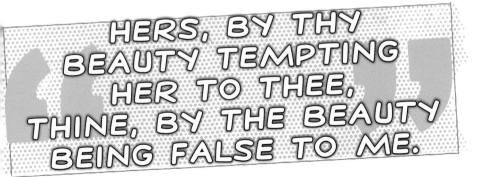

HERS, BY THY BEAUTY TEMPTING HER TO THEE, THINE, BY THE BEAUTY BEING FALSE TO ME.

SONNET 71

No longer mourn for me when I am dead
Than you shall hear the surly sullen bell
Give warning to the world that I am fled
From this vile world, with vilest worms to dwell.   4
Nay, if you read this line, remember not
The hand that writ it, for I love you so
That I in your sweet thoughts would be forgot,
If thinking on me then should make you woe.   8
O, if, I say, you look upon this verse
When I, perhaps, compounded am with clay,
Do not so much as my poor name rehearse,
But let your love even with my life decay,   12
　　Lest the wise world should look into your moan,
　　And mock you with me after I am gone.

PARAPHRASE

Death takes center stage in sonnet 71, one of the most mournful ever written. This sonnet also reflects the speaker's intended selflessness concerning his love for his young friend. The speaker ponders his own death and the effect it will have on his beloved friend. When he dies, he does not want the Fair Youth to feel pain, either from the sadness of the speaker's death or from the memory induced by the poem. The speaker also does not want his friend to mention his name after he dies: he fears that others might mock the younger man because of the speaker's supposedly "poor name," or reputation.

In the first quatrain, with its opening lines leading seamlessly to the period in line 4, the speaker requests that the young man only "mourn" for him at his funeral. The "surly sullen bell" refers to the death bell, a bell rung

SEVERAL WORDS IN SONNET 71, SUCH AS "WOE" AND "MOAN," MIMIC THE LOW TOLLING OF A CHURCH BELL.

THE ORNAMENT OF BEAUTY IS SUSPECT

often before or immediately after a funeral. It told (and tolled) of the death of a parishioner. The bell's "warning" informs the world that the speaker has died and also reminds others of their own mortality. He has left the "vile world" that will mock him after he is gone. The speaker asks his young friend to mourn "no longer" than the bells sound.

The speaker's selflessness surfaces in the second quatrain. Because he loves the Fair Youth so much, he asks him to forget that he even wrote the sonnet. Although the young man's memory of him might consist of "sweet thoughts," the speaker fears that expressing that memory will cause more suffering ("woe").

The third quatrain flows into the couplet, forming a complete thought. These lines direct the young man in his sorrow ("your moan") not to mention the speaker's name once he is decaying in the ground. The speaker speculates on the unreliable value of his own "poor name"—his reputation—after he dies. He fears that mentioning him in public might prompt others to ridicule ("mock") the young man. Therefore, he suggests that the Fair Youth let his love for the speaker die with him.

Ironically, a sonnet so preoccupied with death has become one of the most-quoted and best-known poems ever written, helping to secure Shakespeare's place as one of the greatest writers of the English language.

ANALYSIS

Some scholars have speculated on whether the placement of this sonnet as the seventy-first in the volume was intentional. In Shakespeare's time, a person who lived to be seventy-one would have been considered quite old. Therefore, it seems appropriate for the speaker to speculate on his own mortality in sonnet 71. We have already seen the overwhelming importance of the theme of death and the passage of time.

In general, this sonnet also offers many intriguing contradictions. Can we accept at face value the request by a poet to be forgotten? Can we also accept the request by someone that the one he loves should forget him after he has died? Perhaps this underlying yearning—the unspoken sense that the speaker does not really want to be forgotten in either case—increases the sonnet's overall sadness.

Shakespeare also makes careful use of sound to convey the somber mood of sonnet 71. It is important to remember that a poem is to be *heard* as well as read. Note the repeating *m* sounds in *mourn, worms, remember, compounded, name, moan,* and *mock*. They seem to echo and to extend the melancholy effect of "mourn" in line 1. Thus, through Shakespeare's choice of words, the death bell seems to toll repeatedly in the sonnet's dirgelike sounds.

A great deal of *alliteration* also appears in the poem's lines: the death bell is described as "surly sullen," and in this "vile world" dwell "vilest worms." Once he dies, the speaker says he will be "compounded" with "clay," and he suggests to the young man: "let your love even with my life decay." These instances of repetition add to the overall rhythm throughout the poem. Alliteration also calls attention to the speaker's description of the "wise world" that will mock him after he is gone, thus emphasizing the sarcasm intended in this line.

Sonnets 71 through 74 are part of a quartet dealing specifically with aging and dying. Readers must remember that even if Shakespeare wrote these sonnets in the late 1590s, he was still only in his thirties. Like all the sonnets, they are an artistic creation rather than an autobiography.

SONNET 73

That time of year thou mayst in me behold
When yellow leaves, or none, or few, do hang
Upon those boughs which shake against the cold,
Bare ruined choirs where late the sweet birds sang.   4
In me thou seest the twilight of such day
As after sunset fadeth in the west,
Which by and by black night doth take away,
Death's second self that seals up all in rest.   8
In me thou seest the glowing of such fire
That on the ashes of his youth doth lie,
As the deathbed whereon it must expire,
Consumed with that which it was nourished by.   12
    This thou perceiv'st, which makes thy love more strong,
    To love that well which thou must leave ere long.

PARAPHRASE

Sonnet 73, part of the death quartet, represents the speaker's autumn sonata—his song of aging—told with autumnal images of leafless trees, fading days, and dying fires. Unlike sonnet 71, the speaker's thoughts in sonnet 73 are not speculative: he speaks here as an older man describing what he feels as he ages, acknowledging that life becomes undeniably shorter and more precious.

The first quatrain compares old age to autumn, the "time of year" when trees lose their leaves and birds have flown south. The speaker uses "yellow leaves" and "the cold" to convey the imagery of autumn. With the birds gone, barren trees are compared to empty church choirs.

SONNET 73 NEVER MENTIONS A
SEASON, BUT THE IMAGERY MAKES
IT CLEAR THAT IT IS LATE AUTUMN.

In the following quatrain the speaker describes old age as the "twilight" of the day: the sun has set in the west and is slowly erased by "black night." "Death's second self" is a reference to sleep: as the blackness of night falls, sleep closes up ("seals up") everything else "in rest." The sonnet moves, visually, from the faintest account of color in the yellow leaves to fading twilight to total blackness.

The third quatrain describes the self-consumption of a fire: the more it burns, the more it devours itself. Its "ashes" represent its youth, now gone forever. The growing pile of ashes is the fire's own "deathbed." The fire is fed by the very flames that will eventually put it out, extinguishing it forever. The speaker tells his beloved young friend that looking at the older man will reveal the same effect ("in me thou seest").

The closing couplet tells the young man—and thus the reader—that love is made "more strong" if one perceives that everything one loves, but especially life, is passing. Eventually, all of it "must leave."

ANALYSIS

In sonnet 73 the speaker uses visual imagery in a series of metaphors to convey his message about the transitory aspect of life and the feeling in old age that nothing lasts forever.

In the first quatrain, "yellow leaves," "the cold," and "bare ruined choirs" offer images of autumn to which the speaker compares himself. "Choirs" refer to the part of the church or monastery where services were sung, a reference to the birds singing. Most scholars interpret "ruined" to mean the ruins of Catholic abbeys in Protestant England: many Catholic structures were abandoned or destroyed after the Protestant Reformation. Departed birds once singing in trees before the cold weather arrived are compared to these ruins, in which choristers once sang. Now, all is bare.

The second quatrain follows the movement from dusk, just after the sun sets, to twilight and then to the blackness of night. Through this metaphor the speaker describes himself as being in his own "twilight" and compares "black night" to death coming to take all the light "away." He refers to sleep as "Death's second self," which "seals up" everything "in rest." The speaker compares nighttime to death, or the end of life. Therefore, the day represents youth. The twilight, which marks the end of daytime, is used by the speaker to describe that he is old and nearing death. While night brings a temporary rest to the world, death's rest is final. By using the verb "seals up," Shakespeare brings to mind a coffin, in which a corpse is sealed. The speaker is conscious that he is moving toward death.

In the third quatrain the speaker compares the dilemma of aging to the self-consuming quality of a fire. In this extended metaphor the fire's "youth" is compared to the speaker's younger years, now reduced to ashes. As one ages, youth is "consumed" in the act of living and the passage of time. Therefore, it becomes its own "deathbed." The use of "expire" (which means "to die") reinforces the speaker's message. The fire feeds on itself just as life leads inevitably to death. The third metaphor imparts a more final feeling than the first two. Spring may follow autumn, and day may follow night—but an extinguished fire is gone for good.

Line 12 ("Consumed with that which it was nourished by"), scholars have pointed out, succinctly sums up the progress of life from beginning to end.

THE WORTH OF THAT IS THAT WHICH IT CONTAINS

In the closing couplet the speaker reaffirms that his friend can see these things ("thou perceiv'st") by stating directly that the younger man can perceive his basic point: one must love strongly that which he knows will soon be gone. One might also interpret the final lines as a warning to the young friend (or the reader) to cherish what one loves in this life. Like the speaker's youth, one day it too will be gone.

SONNET 95

How sweet and lovely dost thou make the shame
Which, like a canker in the fragrant rose,
Doth spot the beauty of thy budding name!
O, in what sweets dost thou thy sins enclose!   4
That tongue that tells the story of thy days
Making lascivious comments on thy sport,
Cannot dispraise but in a kind of praise;
Naming thy name blesses an ill report.   8
O, what a mansion have those vices got
Which for their habitation chose out thee,
Where beauty's veil doth cover every blot,
And all things turns to fair that eyes can see!   12
    Take heed, dear heart, of this large privilege;
    The hardest knife ill used doth lose his edge.

PARAPHRASE

Sonnet 95 is one of five (92 to 96) in which the speaker criticizes his young friend and questions his virtue. In this sonnet of admonishment, the speaker takes the Fair Youth to task for his public behavior, which is apparently earning him a bad reputation. Still, the speaker cannot help but praise the young man's beauty at the same time that he criticizes his behavior.

The SICK ROSE

O Rose, thou art sick.
The invisible worm,
That flies in the night
In the howling storm:

Has found out thy bed
Of crimson joy:
And his dark secret love
Does thy life destroy.

A ROSE DAMAGED BY A WORM WAS A POPULAR POETIC IMAGE. WILLIAM BLAKE WROTE AND ILLUSTRATED "THE SICK ROSE," WHICH WAS PUBLISHED AS PART OF A 1794 POETRY COLLECTION.

In the first quatrain the speaker compares the Fair Youth to a rose that looks and smells wonderful but hides "a canker," which refers to a worm that eats and destroys a flower, leaving a decaying spot. In a rose, this occurs while the flower is still closed as a bud and does not become obvious until it has opened. Therefore, the speaker tells the young man that he is ruining his good (and "budding") name. Still, the speaker cannot help but comment on the sweet and lovely package that contains those "sins." This disconnect between the young man's fair looks and his questionable behavior runs throughout these five sonnets.

In the second quatrain the speaker attempts to warn the young man about his reputation. Even the public's wagging "tongue"—speaking in sexual innuendo ("lascivious") about the young man's social escapades (his "sport")—cannot completely insult ("dispraise") him. By merely mentioning the Fair Youth's name, the public "blesses" its own gossip ("ill report") about him—speaking about him turns the public's gossip into a blessing.

In the third quatrain the speaker does not deny his young friend has "vices." Yet he does insist that they have chosen to reside in a beautiful home ("a mansion"). The speaker observes that the young friend's attractiveness ("beauty's veil") covers up every spot, recalling the earlier image of the "canker" that "spot[s]" the rose. When people look at the Fair Youth, his behavior, no matter how full of vices, turns "fair."

In the closing couplet the speaker warns his young friend that beauty grants someone a great deal of freedom ("privilege"), which the Fair Youth seems to be enjoying. Still, the speaker adds that even the sharpest knife, if used incorrectly, will eventually lose its edge.

ANALYSIS

Sonnet 95 offers a fine example of Shakespeare's skill in playing with the more established conventions of love poetry. Throughout literature, the rose often appears as a symbol of perfection. Whereas the rose is traditionally

HOW LIKE EVE'S APPLE DOTH THY BEAUTY GROW.

used to express love and beauty, the speaker uses the rose to point out the Fair Youth's "shame." He employs a simile comparing that shame to the "spot" caused by a canker in a rose: the rose may still smell sweet, but it is diseased from within. The beloved friend's shame—his behavior—has had a similar effect on his reputation.

The use of "tongue" in line 5 offers an example of metonymy in which the tongue represents the gossip that has spread about the young man's wild behavior. The metaphor in line 9 compares the Fair Youth's body to an elegant mansion that nevertheless houses vices. The veil of beauty—the young man's looks—hides every flaw ("cover every blot"), making all of his behavior seem "fair." The speaker's beloved friend is young and still "budding": we can recall that the spot on the rose does not reveal itself until the flower opens—and then it is too late. The damage has been done.

Rhetorically, the speaker appears to move some of the blame away from his young friend. By saying that the Fair Youth's vices "chose" him, the speaker subtly transfers responsibility for his friend's behavior to an outside force. He closes with a heartfelt ("dear heart") warning to the young man in the proverbial statement that a knife will lose its edge if misused. Some scholars see a sexual pun in the use of "hardest knife" as a possible reference to the young friend's penis. The pun emphasizes the speaker's concern for his young friend's irresponsible sexual escapades. Although his wild behavior may be soiling his reputation, the Fair Youth remains beautiful to the speaker.

Let me not to the marriage of true minds
Admit impediments; love is not love
Which alters when it alteration finds,
Or bends with the remover to remove.   4
O, no, it is an ever-fixèd mark
That looks on tempests and is never shaken;
It is the star to every wand'ring bark,
Whose worth's unknown, although his height be taken. 8
Love's not Time's fool, though rosy lips and cheeks
Within his bending sickle's compass come;
Love alters not with brief hours and weeks,
But bears it out even to the edge of doom.   12
    If this be error, and upon me proved,
    I never writ, nor no man ever loved.

PARAPHRASE

Sonnet 116 is one of the most famous and most frequently quoted poems written in the English language. To many, it represents a paean—a song of praise—to the enduring quality of true love; to others it is a valentine to the depth of real friendship, especially between two men. Shakespeare uses persuasive arguments and carefully chosen metaphors to present the sonnet's messages about the unchanging nature of genuine love. The sonnet's wonderful rhythm and unforgettable imagery play as important a role as the speaker's theme.

In the first quatrain the speaker employs language taken from the Christian marriage ceremony in which the minister asks the couple if either of them knows of any "impediments" that would stop the marriage from taking place. The speaker insists he will not admit that any obstacles exist when it comes to the love between two "true" people. Love, he argues, cannot be love if it changes ("alters") every time a change occurs in a person or a situation. Love neither "bends" nor gives in every time someone in a relationship decides to withdraw ("remove"). In other words, love will not leave with the leaver.

In the next quatrain—which the speaker begins with "O, no" to emphasize his certainty in his assertions about love—he compares love to a "mark" at sea: a marker such as a beacon or geographical feature or some building that sailors use for guidance. The mark is "fixèd" because it never moves and is reliable. The speaker then compares love to the star on which sailors on a ship ("wand'ring bark") rely to help them find their way. The star may also refer to the North Star, which Shakespeare calls "constant" in his play *Julius Caesar*. The value ("worth") of such an important star is immeasurable—even if one could work out its altitude (the star's "height").

In the third quatrain the speaker returns to one of his favorite subjects: the destructive nature of time. Time's "bending sickle" is a reference to the allegorical figure of Death, who carries a sickle with which he chops down life. The speaker argues that rosy lips and cheeks—both emblems of youth—may fall victim to Time's sickle, but not love. Love refuses to change ("alters") in the face of Time's "brief hours and weeks." Instead, love endures—it persists—even to the end of time ("the edge of doom"). In this case "doom" may also refer to the Last Judgment, a reference we also saw in sonnet 55.

ANALYSIS

A wonderful contrast exists in this sonnet between its emotional subject matter—the nature of true love—and the very rational, methodical arguments used to present the poet's thoughts. In his book *The World of Shakespeare's Sonnets*, Robert Matz contends that the subject of this sonnet is male friendship rather than romantic love: "In sonnet 116 male friendship takes the place of marriage, which provides a metaphor for friendship." From this point of view, the poet's logical-sounding arguments seem more applicable to the deep bond between two friends. "The marriage" of sonnet 116 occurs between "true minds."

The speaker begins by stating that he simply will not allow any obstacles in this "marriage of true minds." If he refers specifically to his connection to the Fair Youth, he appears to be saying that no change in his young friend will ever alter his love for him. He argues that change—in the form of "alters" and "alteration"—cannot threaten true love, or else it would not be love.

Metaphors drive the second quatrain in which the poet compares genuine love to two objects: a permanent landmark ("an ever-fixèd mark") that guides ships through "tempests" and a star guiding every traveling ship ("wand'ring bark"). The speaker compares real love to a star that can never really be measured ("Whose worth's unknown") because the star is too distant. Still, love functions as a guiding force in the course of one's life.

As in so many other sonnets, Shakespeare personifies time and casts it as the villain in sonnet 116. Time's "sickle" recalls the allegorical figure of Death, often depicted with a scythe in his hands. "Rosy lips and cheeks" function as metonymies for youthful beauty. They may come within the range ("compass") of Time's destructive scythe, yet Time will have no effect on love. The speaker calls Time's hours and weeks "brief," another of the sonnet's many references to the rapid passage of time and its negative effect. However, love will not change as time passes: the speaker argues that love will endure ("bears it out") even to the end of time.

The speaker closes this sonnet with legal language: "If this be error, and upon me proved, / I never writ, nor no man ever loved." The speaker argues that everything he has said must be proven ("proved") to be an error. A writ of error is a written order issued by a court and used to reverse a legal judgment on the ground of error. In a pun Shakespeare then plays on the idea of such a writ by using the word in another meaning—as the past tense of "to write": "I never writ." A facetious tone also surfaces in the final couplet as the speaker argues: if what I've just said is proven untrue, then no one has ever loved—and I have never been a writer. Who would argue with such a claim?

SONNET 129

Th' expense of spirit in a waste of shame
Is lust in action; and, till action, lust
Is perjured, murd'rous, bloody, full of blame,
Savage, extreme, rude, cruel, not to trust;   4
Enjoyed no sooner but despised straight;
Past reason hunted, and no sooner had,
Past reason hated as a swallowed bait
On purpose laid to make the taker mad: 8
Mad in pursuit, and in possession so;
Had, having, and in quest to have, extreme;
A bliss in proof, and proved, a very woe;
Before, a joy proposed; behind, a dream.   12
        All this the world well knows, yet none knows well
        To shun the heaven that leads men to this hell.

PARAPHRASE

Sonnet 129 comes from Shakespeare's second sonnet sequence, which deals with the speaker's affair with the mysterious Dark Lady. In *William Shakespeare: The Complete Works* it is noted that these sonnets "depict an illicit, intense, and far from ennobling passion for an unworthy woman." We know very little about the Dark Lady—or if she actually existed—but she is a marvelous creation because she is different from the typical female object of worship found in most sonnet sequences. Instead of beautiful, virginal, and good, the Dark Lady is depicted as unattractive, unfaithful, and dishonest.

Sonnet 129 opens with some negative thoughts on the power of lust. The speaker looks at lust from three angles: when one feels lust, when one acts on lust, and the feelings one has after acting on lust.

He first comments on lust's power to drive people to want something intensely, only to despise it once it is over. In lust, the speaker claims, a person expends a lot of energy ("spirit") in an act that only results in wasting that very energy. Afterward, one finds oneself in a wasteland of "shame." This, the speaker says, is "lust in action." Until one acts on lust, it is false ("perjured") and likely to kill and maim—perhaps metaphorically murdering innocence. These feelings leave one racked with guilt: "full of blame" (3). The speaker warns that feelings of lust can be savage ("rude, cruel") and should not be trusted.

In the second quatrain the speaker indicates that as soon as lust is enjoyed it becomes "despised." Lust is eagerly and irrationally pursued, yet once it is had, it is just as vehemently "hated." Lust is like bait, intentionally left to trap a person into behaving irrationally.

Therefore, in the third quatrain the speaker claims that one is "mad" when pursuing lust and just as mad when possessing it. In all three stages lust is extreme: when one tries to fulfill lust ("in quest"), while someone is "having" it, and once it is over. Lust may be blissful when one is trying it out ("in proof"), but once it has been tried ("proved") the same bliss turns into "woe." Before one fulfills his passion, lust is a "joy" one looks forward to; yet once it is over ("behind"), lust becomes only a delusion ("a dream").

In the closing couplet the speaker admits that everyone "knows" all about these negative aspects of lust, but no one is strong enough to avoid

MARY FITTON, A MEMBER OF QUEEN ELIZABETH'S COURT, IS BELIEVED BY SOME SCHOLARS TO BE SHAKESPEARE'S DARK LADY.

("shun") it. In a clever turn of phrase, the speaker concludes that lust is a "heaven"—a promise of bliss—that only "leads men to hell."

ANALYSIS

Throughout this thoughtful sonnet, Shakespeare sets up a contrast between the power of lust before one satisfies it and the feelings one is left with after fulfilling it. The language is full of clever puns that would have been more readily recognized in Shakespeare's time. The word "spirit," for example, can refer to energy—but in Shakespeare's day it was also another way of referring to semen. The speaker claims that sexual energy is "waste[d]" when lust is "in action."

The speaker employs a list of words with negative connotations when describing lust before it is acted upon: *perjured, murd'rous, bloody, blame, savage, extreme, rude,* and *cruel.* The sequences and short phrases appearing in this sonnet add to its rhythmic effect.

In the second quatrain the speaker creates an extended metaphor, comparing lust to hunting. In lust one hunts for the object of passion "past reason"—irrationally. But after one takes the bait, one is just as irrationally "mad" about it. The trap has been laid "on purpose" for this very reason: to drive the taker "mad." The use of "laid" is surely another sexual pun. In this sense, the hunter gets captured by the game.

Shakespeare cleverly keeps the sonnet moving by repeating "Mad" at the beginning of the third quatrain. In her book *The Art of Shakespeare's Sonnets,* scholar Helen Vendler points out that this poem "presents us with two models of experience, both of which we know intimately: the model of 'What I think of it now that I look back' and the model of 'How it felt while it was happening.'" This is specifically referenced in the "had" and "having" in line 10.

Although much "joy" exists when one is in anticipation of fulfilling desires, one is left afterward with nothing but "a dream." The speaker does not seem to be speaking about lust within a loving relationship but about lust for its own sake. In other sonnets (see sonnets 141 and 142, for example), he refers to his relationship with the Dark Lady as "sin."

An impersonal tone pervades this sonnet, which seems more like a commentary on lust and a warning than a personal statement of feelings. Notice that neither "I" nor "thou" appears in this poem. Within the sonnet sequence the speaker is in the middle of his affair with the Dark Lady, and one senses he feels regret about having succumbed to his physical desires for her. Thanks to pursuing some heavenly moments, he is in "hell" because of his current feelings of regret. Readers will notice the difference in tone and approach from the first 126 sonnets to the Fair Youth. The adulterous nature of the speaker's affair with the Dark Lady obviously colors his response to that relationship.

SONNET 130

My mistress' eyes are nothing like the sun;
Coral is far more red than her lips' red;
If snow be white, why then her breasts are dun;
If hairs be wires, black wires grow on her head.   4
I have seen roses damasked, red and white,
But no such roses see I in her cheeks;
And in some perfumes is there more delight
Than in the breath that from my mistress reeks.   8
I love to hear her speak; yet well I know
That music hath a far more pleasing sound:
I grant I never saw a goddess go;
My mistress, when she walks, treads on the ground.   12
    And yet, by heaven, I think my love as rare
    As any she belied with false compare.

In sonnet 130 the speaker takes a realistic look at his mistress and finds that she does not live up to the standard comparisons applied to most women who are the subjects of sonnets. Unlike many of the objects of affection praised in most of the sonnets, the Dark Lady is not blond, nor pink skinned, nor sweet breathed.

In the first quatrain the speaker lists standard similes applied to beautiful women loved from afar by sonneteers—and informs us that his mistress lacks all of these qualities. Her eyes are not as bright as the sun, and her lips are not as red as coral. Her skin is neither fair nor white (no comparisons to snow or alabaster here!). In fact, the skin of her breasts is a "dun" color: a dull, brownish gray. Whereas most sonnet writers praise the beautiful blond hair of their subjects, often referring to it as golden wires, the speaker compares his mistress's hair to "black wires."

The rose appears in a number of the sonnets, but the second quatrain tells us that beautiful roses of red and white are not found in his lover's cheeks. Also, if he is looking for beautiful scents he will have to try perfumes and forget his mistress's breath, which "reeks." In the third quatrain the speaker admits that, while he "love[s]" to hear his mistress speak, the sound is not as "pleasing" as music. And, even if he has never seen a goddess walk (goddesses' feet supposedly never touched the ground), he can safely say that his lover's feet are firmly planted "on the ground."

O, NEVER SAY THAT I WAS FALSE OF HEART.

The closing couplet comes almost as surprise, as the speaker informs us that despite all these apparent flaws he loves his mistress and finds her as "rare" as any woman whom other poets have misrepresented ("belied") with a flowery comparison ("false compare"). The speaker loves a mistress who is a real woman, not an idealized beauty.

ANALYSIS

Sonnet 130 has become one of Shakespeare's most famous and enjoyed. It is an antisonnet. The poem uses traditional similes to seemingly insult the Dark Lady but does, in fact, praise her. Scholars often call this sonnet "anti-Petrarchan," because it breaks free from the standard worship of a fair woman that Petrarch established in the fourteenth century. Sonnet 130 offers a parody—a humorous imitation—of Petrarch's highly romantic sonnets to his beloved Laura. Even in Shakespeare's time poets were still writing sonnets to idealized portraits of unattainable women.

Some scholars view Shakespeare's attitude in sonnet 130 as misogynistic, or hateful toward women. Yet a closer reading of the poem reveals that what look like insults are simply statements of facts. The Dark Lady is not a pure beauty beyond the speaker's reach; she is, instead, a real breathing woman with flaws. Music may sound lovelier than her voice, and maybe she does not walk on air like a goddess. Still, he finds her as rare as any of the idealized women to whom other poets have written.

The poet emphasizes his final opinion in the use of "I think." His description of those other women who receive "false compare" seems like an insult directed at the dishonesty of those poets who over-praise the women they love. The fault lies not in his mistress but in the exaggerated, false comparisons made by other poets. Readers will notice that the speaker used more idealized words when describing the Fair Youth.

SONNET 144

Two loves I have, of comfort and despair,
Which like two spirits do suggest me still:
The better angel is a man right fair;
The worser spirit a woman coloured ill.   4
To win me soon to hell my female evil
Tempteth my better angel from my side,
And would corrupt my saint to be a devil,
Wooing his purity with her foul pride.   8
And whether that my angel be turned fiend
Suspect I may, yet not directly tell,
But being both from me, both to each friend,
I guess one angel in another's hell.   12
    Yet this shall I ne'er know, but live in doubt,
    Till my bad angel fire my good one out.

PARAPHRASE

In sonnet 144 the speaker presents the seduction of the Fair Youth by a person most scholars believe is the Dark Lady. In the first quatrain the speaker refers to his two lovers as "comfort and despair." He says that the two loves are like two angels, or "spirits," who are always prompting him to do something: "suggest me still." He then defines the two angels as a "fair" man and a woman of dark color ("coloured ill").

In the second quatrain the speaker observes that the second angel—his "female evil"—wants to win him over "to hell." Therefore, she seduces ("Tempteth") his fair friend—his "better angel"—away from him. She wants to corrupt his good angel ("my saint") into a devil by "wooing" him away from his goodness ("purity").

In the third quatrain the speaker says he can only speculate on what is happening. He suspects that his good angel has been turned into a devil ("fiend"), but the speaker cannot be certain. Because his two friends are both away from him ("from me"), he can only "guess" that the good angel has been seduced into hell. The couplet reinforces the speaker's uncertainty: he will never really know what has happened between the Dark Lady and the Fair Youth until the bad angel finally rejects the good one.

ANALYSIS

Throughout this sonnet, Shakespeare employs the conventional Christian image of a good and a bad angel vying for control of someone's soul. Yet, as the simile ("like two spirits") suggests, the speaker's intentions are more personal than theological. He believes that the Dark Lady has seduced the Fair Youth, and he views it as a betrayal by both of his friends.

As many of the sonnets reveal, the speaker has found mostly comfort with the Fair Youth and mostly despair in his relationship with the Dark Lady—although both aspects appear in various sonnets. *Comfort and despair* are also theological terms meaning "salvation" and "damnation," respectively. At the sonnet's start, the speaker seems convinced that his "worser" angel is seducing his "better" angel away from him.

In the first line of the second stanza the speaker claims that the woman is trying to seduce him "to hell," which was slang for "vagina" in Renaissance England. The Dark Lady, whom the speaker calls his "female evil," lures the young man with her "foul pride," a reference to sexual heat. On the other

> ALL MEN ARE BAD AND IN THEIR BADNESS REIGN.

hand, the speaker describes the Fair Youth as "my saint" who possesses "purity." Sexist notions that women are the source of evil seem to surface in these descriptions.

The speaker's uncertainty about the relationship between the Fair Youth and the Dark Lady marks the language of the last six lines. The speaker is unsure whether his young friend has become a "fiend" (9) by surrendering to the bad angel's seduction. Still, he guesses that it has happened. Another sexual pun on "hell" occurs in line 12: "I guess one angel in another's hell." However, in the couplet the speaker says he can never really know—he can only "live in doubt." Scholars have interpreted the final line in a number of ways. Perhaps she finally rejects the young man and blasts him off to hell and its eternal fires. The "fire" of line 14 may also refer to venereal disease and the inflammation the young man would experience if he contracted it.

SONNET 147

My love is as a fever, longing still
For that which longer nurseth the disease.
Feeding on that which doth preserve the ill,
Th' uncertain sickly appetite to please.   4
My reason, the physician to my love,
Angry that his prescriptions are not kept,
Hath left me, and I desperate now approve
Desire is death, which physic did except.   8
Past cure I am, now reason is past care,
And frantic-mad with evermore unrest;
My thoughts and my discourse as madmen's are,
At random from the truth vainly expressed: 12
    For I have sworn thee fair, and thought thee bright,
    Who art as black as hell, as dark as night.

In sonnet 147 the speaker compares his affection for his mistress to a disease that has taken over his entire existence. His physician, reason, has left him and the speaker has declared himself "past cure." His tortured love for the Dark Lady has finally driven him mad.

In the first quatrain the speaker compares his love to a fever that compels him to long for the very thing that is making him sick. The more he longs for his love, the "longer" it nurtures and prolongs his disease, preventing his recovery. Because his love feeds on itself, it "preserve[s]" the illness. Therefore, in his lovesickness he desires to "please" his love, which causes his fever to continue. The speaker finds himself caught in a vicious cycle.

In the second quatrain the speaker describes his reason as a physician who has given up on his patient. Because the doctor is "angry" that his patient has not followed his recommendations ("prescriptions"), he has abandoned this man who is sick with love. Trapped in a desperate state, the speaker proves by his experience that "Desire" is, indeed, death. Although the physician had forbidden that desire—"which physic did except"—the speaker would not listen.

The speaker moves toward madness in the third quatrain. Because his reason—the physician—has left him, the speaker is "past cure." He has become "frantic-mad" with an "unrest" that will not end. His thoughts and his speech resemble those of a madman: they are wandering insanely ("at random") from the truth and are expressed without purpose ("vainly").

In the couplet the poet speaks directly to his mistress. He tells her he believed her to be "fair" and "bright," but in reality she is neither good nor beautiful.

ANALYSIS

Sonnet 147, one of Shakespeare's darkest, offers us a poetic glimpse into the mind of a man whose desire has destroyed his well-being. As the sonnet

I WILL BE TRUE DESPITE THY SCYTHE AND THEE.

progresses, the speaker moves from illness to an incurable state and finally to madness. The reason is quite simple: he has lost his own reason—the common sense that would have stopped him from continuing to pursue his desires.

The opening simile comparing the speaker's desire to a fever sets the tone. At first the speaker appears to be a man who is delirious—in a "fever"—with love. Shakespeare cleverly plays on the word "longing" in the first line by using "longer" in the second, thereby extending the overall sense of desire. Desire becomes a disease: it feeds on itself, prolonging the illness merely to please the speaker's desire. Because he never knows when his desire will arise, he describes it as "uncertain" (4). In the initial quatrain Shakespeare makes the reader feel the hopelessness of the situation. His word choice reinforces the overall comparison: *fever, disease, ill, sickly*.

A metaphor follows in the next quatrain as the speaker compares his reason—his rational sense—to a physician tending to the speaker's "love." Unfortunately, the doctor has left. Having become a slave to his own desires, the speaker would not listen to his own reason. Rationality, the speaker claims, leaves when one is trapped in the vicious cycle of longing for what one should not want. In this hopeless situation, "Desire" can only lead to death: his passion has become deadly.

The first line of the third quatrain—"Past cure I am, now reason is past care"—is an allusion to an old proverb: "Past cure is past care." Because reason (his physician) does not care any longer, it has abandoned the

SONNETS ARE TRADITIONALLY CONSIDERED TO BE ROMANTIC. THIS NINETEENTH-CENTURY PAINTING DEPICTS A YOUNG MAN TRYING TO WIN THE WOMAN'S AFFECTION BY WRITING HER A SONNET.

speaker. Therefore, he cannot be cured. Shakespeare also puns on "care," which can refer either to being under the care of a doctor or to caring or worrying about something. Once the speaker's reason leaves, it sets the stage for his madness. He claims that his thoughts and his speech reveal that he has lost all sense of the truth, and he finds himself in a frantic state of unrest. Shakespeare chooses words with strong connotations of unease: *frantic-mad*, *unrest*, *madmen*. The sonnet imparts the speaker's feelings to the reader.

An abrupt shift occurs in the closing couplet, in which the speaker seems to regain his clarity. He directs his statements to his mistress, and his anger is apparent. Realizing he has been mistaken about her, the speaker uses standard imagery ("black as hell" and "dark as night") with negative connotations to describe her. The darkness also alludes to her coloring, reminding us that the object of the speaker's desire is not the classic fair-haired beauty of most sonnet sequences. Of course, the implication of the mistress's impurity is not to be disregarded.

The speaker must be aware that he is being irrational since he comments that his thoughts resemble those of a madman. As Vendler observes: "The paradox of the sonnet is that this 'madman' is perfectly clear about what the truth is: he knows that his thoughts and his discourse are 'at random from *the truth*.'" Has his reason left him—or does he knowingly refuse to listen to it?

GIVE THEM THY FINGERS, ME THY LIPS TO KISS.

SHAKESPEARE EXPLAINED: THE SONNETS

A LOVE TRIANGLE: CHARACTERS IN THE SONNETS

THE SPEAKER

Although many readers assume that the speaker of the sonnets is Shakespeare, he may well have created a fictional voice that speaks through these poems. Either way, a distinct character slowly emerges in the sonnets. Like Shakespeare, the speaker makes his living as a writer. We also learn that he is a middle-aged man or one who is definitely older than the Fair Youth. In sonnet 62 he refers to his own face as "chopped with tanned antiquity," and in sonnet 73 he describes his "time of year" as autumn. Through many of his comments, the speaker reveals that he is of lower social status than his beloved young friend. He also appears to be a poet looking for a patron to support his writing career.

One of the first character traits that the speaker reveals is his selfless nature. The speaker of the sonnets claims repeatedly that he wants only what is best for the Fair Youth. He urges him to marry and to have children, and he asks his young friend to forget him when the speaker dies for fear that the world might mock the young man. In sonnet 39 the speaker tells us that the Fair Youth represents his "better part" (2). The speaker finds separation from the Fair Youth to be unbearable, revealing a strong emotional attachment that seems undeniably romantic. His words also indicate a somewhat jealous nature—especially when another speaker vies for the young man's attention (see sonnets 78 to 86).

When portraying his relationship with the Dark Lady (sonnets 127 to 152), the speaker's language becomes much more aggressive. He often criticizes his mistress for her behavior and makes a number of sexual puns. In sonnet 147 he compares their relationship to a "sickly appetite." Sonnet 152 implies that the speaker is married ("I am forsworn"); therefore, he is having an affair with his dark mistress. Sonnet 144 also reveals that the Dark Lady has had an affair with the Fair Youth, leaving the poet caught in a love triangle.

Sonnets 135, 136, and 143 indicate that the speaker's first name is "Will," and he makes a number of puns based on it. In sonnet 136 the speaker tells us: "for my name is Will" (14). Readers must decide for themselves if that is a direct indication that the "I" of the sonnets is Shakespeare.

THE FAIR YOUTH

Over the centuries, much speculation has surrounded the identity of the young friend who is the object of the speaker's affection in the first 126 sonnets. A number of critics have tried to guess his identity, thanks in great part to the dedication to a "Mr. W.H." that appears at the beginning of the sonnets. Possibilities include two of Shakespeare's patrons: Henry Wriothesley, the Earl of Southampton, and William Herbert, the Earl of Pembroke. However, the figure that emerges from the sonnet seems more like a literary creation, an object of worship and affection. Scholar Douglas Bush points out that "Shakespeare's young man, like a Petrarchan mistress, is more loved than loving." Perhaps he is a compilation of many people.

Throughout the poems the speaker refers to the young man as "youth," "sweet boy," and "friend," and in sonnet 37 we learn that he possesses "beauty," "birth," "wealth," and "wit." We know that the young man is of high social status—a possible patron for the speaker. At some point, the young friend seems to have insulted or hurt the speaker. In sonnets 35 and 41 the speaker says he forgives the Fair Youth for something he has done. And in sonnet 120 the speaker reveals that he has also hurt his young friend.

Men in Shakespeare's time often declared their feelings for each other. In the first seventeen sonnets the speaker urges the young man to marry (though some scholars have found these arguments of persuasion unconvincing). In sonnet 20 the speaker compares the young man to a woman: he describes him as having "a woman's face" and calls him "the master mistress of my passion." Yet, in the same sonnet, the speaker refers to the young man's penis as "one thing" that adds "nothing" to the speaker's "purpose." The sonnets reveal no clear signs of the Fair Youth's feelings for the speaker. Modern readers must also remember that people in Shakespeare's time did not define themselves by their sexual activity.

THE DARK LADY

The speaker never actually refers to the other main character who appears in the sonnets by the name history has given her: the Dark Lady. She is a mysterious woman of dark complexion and hair coloring whom the speaker often refers to as his "mistress." Her appearance is in stark contrast to the idealistic fair—blond—beauty that most sonneteers describe in their poems. Certain lines indicate that the Dark Lady is married, making her an adulterer; and others actually imply that she has a venereal disease.

The twenty-six sonnets addressed to the Dark Lady reveal the speaker's strong feelings for her, and they also indicate his torment over having those feelings. In sonnet 131 the speaker calls his mistress "tyrannous," and

"THEN WILL I SWEAR BEAUTY HERSELF IS BLACK."

Principum   amicitias!

THIS PORTRAIT, WHICH MADE ITS PUBLIC DEBUT IN 2009, IS THOUGHT TO BE THE ONLY AUTHENTIC IMAGE OF SHAKESPEARE MADE DURING HIS LIFE. ACCORDING TO ART HISTORIANS IT WAS PAINTED AROUND 1610.

in a number of sonnets he indicates that she has been untrue. Her false nature becomes a major concern throughout the sonnets written about her. At one point she seems to seduce the Fair Youth, dealing the speaker a double betrayal by both his friend and his mistress. The speaker also uses surprisingly sexual language to describe his affair with the Dark Lady.

The Dark Lady's deceptions seem to reflect the speaker's self-deception about his feelings for her. In sonnet 138 the speaker explains that his mistress swears she is "made of truth" when they both know she lies. At the same time, he convinces himself that she thinks he is still "young," and she happily plays along. Therefore they "lie" together—all puns intended!—and flatter each other in their lies.

Scholars have long speculated on the identity of the Dark Lady (if there is one). Some believe she was Lucy Morgan, a dark-skinned woman who was a well-known London brothel keeper. Morgan was also a courtesan (a prostitute who socialized with men of high position). Others believe the Dark Lady was actually Mary Fitton, a lady-in-waiting in Queen Elizabeth's court who had an affair with the Earl of Pembroke. The woman we meet in the sonnets may well be a compilation of many women, a puzzling figure representing the sometimes difficult nature of romantic love between a man and a woman.

A CLOSER LOOK

- THEMES

- MOTIFS

- SYMBOLS

- LANGUAGE

- INTERPRETING THE SONNETS

A late sixteenth-century ▶
illustration of a courting couple.
This image portrays a more
idealistic romance than that in
many of Shakespeare's sonnets.

Chapter
Three

66929
66929

CHAPTER THREE

a Closer Look

THEMES

THE DESTRUCTIVE NATURE OF TIME

If there is a "villain" who appears in the sonnets, particularly in those addressed to the Fair Youth, it is Time. Throughout the sonnets, Time appears as a destructive force that ravages youthful beauty. Shakespeare often capitalizes *Time*, emphasizing that it is a symbolic or allegorical figure. For example, in sonnet 16 he refers to "this bloody tyrant, Time" (2). In sonnet 19 the speaker directly addresses "Devouring Time" (19) and warns it not to commit the "heinous crime" (8) of aging the Fair Youth.

The speaker recognizes the unstoppable nature of time: everything eventually changes and dies. In sonnet 15 he describes a debate between "wasteful Time" and "Decay" (11) in which the two symbolic figures plot to destroy the young friend's "youth." In sonnets 2 and 12 the speaker suggests that his beloved can overcome time by having children. In sonnet 12 he claims that nothing else can "make defence" against "Time's scythe" (13)—the scythe cuts down everything in its path. In sonnet 64 the speaker admits that eventually "Time will come and take my love away" (12).

Through his poetry the speaker attempts to defy Time. He hopes that his verse will endure and keep alive the beautiful nature of his young friend—despite the passing of time. In sonnet 18 he refers to the "eternal lines" (12) of poetry that he hopes will preserve for all time the memory of the Fair Youth. In sonnet 123 the speaker tells "Time" directly that his feelings will not change: "I will be true, despite thy scythe and thee" (14). As the speaker writes in sonnet 100, he believes his poems will grant lasting fame to his beloved "faster than Time wastes life" (13).

THE SELFLESS SIDE OF LOVE

Throughout many of the sonnets—and especially those addressed to the Fair Youth—the speaker discusses his love in selfless terms. The speaker frequently plays down his own self-worth in favor of elevating the Fair Youth, and many of these sonnets seem to present love as one-sided. In sonnet 26, for example, the speaker describes his affection for his young friend as a kind of "vassalage" (1), a term from feudal times referring to the allegiance one owes a superior. In the same sonnet, the speaker views himself in the "duty" (4, 5) of his beloved.

This emotional battle between what is best for the lover and what is best for the beloved is a common one in Renaissance poetry. In sonnet 37 the speaker compares himself to a "decrepit father" who "takes delight" in an active child. Sonnet 87 reveals that the speaker believes his young friend is "too dear for my possessing" (1). In sonnet 91 the speaker admits that his friend's love "is better than high birth" to him (9), and in sonnet 109 he tells his young friend: "thou art my all" (14). These descriptions reinforce the selfless—rather than selfish—nature of love.

If the poet has written these sonnets specifically for a patron, his selflessness may well have another purpose: to flatter his patron and to keep his support. In sonnet 103 the speaker claims that the Fair Youth's beauty—his face in the mirror—is greater than the "blunt invention" (or dull creation) (7) of the speaker's verses: "And more, much more, than in my verse can sit / Your own glass shows you when you look in it" (13–14). The speaker is even willing to insult his own poetry in favor of the young friend's beauty. As he claims in sonnet 39, the Fair Youth is "the better part of" the speaker (2). Praising the young man, the speaker says, is praising himself.

THE FICKLE HAND OF FORTUNE

In Shakespeare's time many people believed that supernatural forces influenced and controlled their lives. In poetry and drama this force is often personified as Fortune, a figure that serves a symbolic or allegorical function. Within this worldview, misfortune becomes the whim of Fate. In sonnet 37 the speaker observes that he has been "made lame by Fortune's dearest spite" (3)—he has had to suffer losses because of chance misfortunes. In sonnet 29 the speaker tells us that when he is "in disgrace with Fortune" (1), he only needs to think on his beloved friend to feel he has great "wealth" (13).

Stars often function as a symbol of fortune and fate in Renaissance writing. In sonnet 14 the speaker tells his lover, "Not from the stars do I my judgment pluck, / And yet methinks I have astronomy" (1–2). Although the speaker does not take his opinions ("judgment") from the stars, he believes he knows and understands astrology (referred to as "astronomy"). Still, he is not looking to discern his future from the skies; the stars to which the speaker refers are his beloved's "eyes," which he calls "constant stars" (10). In sonnet 26 the speaker says that he waits for the "star" that will "guide" him to the kind of success that will make him worthy of the Fair Youth (9). The speaker suggests, in sonnet 111, that the Fair Youth should argue with Fortune about the speaker's "public" (4) state of affairs. Blame Fortune, the speaker says, not me.

In sonnet 124 the speaker insists that his love for his friend is not an accident or a product of chance. If it were, he says, it would be "Fortune's bastard" (2). Instead, the speaker says that his love was built "far from accident" (5). In this sonnet the speaker attempts to place his love outside the realm of Fortune or chance.

THE CONFLICT BETWEEN REASON AND PASSION

Especially in the sonnets written about the Dark Lady, Shakespeare focuses on the conflict between reason and passion. In sonnet 148 the speaker asks, "where is my judgment fled" (3)? His common sense—his reason—seems to escape him when dealing with his feelings for his mistress. Instead, love keeps him "blind" (13) to her faults: his passion overcomes his reason. In sonnet 150 the speaker points out that he has many "just" reasons to "hate" the Dark Lady, yet her "unworthiness" has "raised love" in him (13). The speaker seems unable to control his passion and feelings, even though his rational mind tells him to do otherwise.

Sonnet 138 implies that the speaker's love for his dark mistress is based solely on lies, although he is aware of them. She lies and says she is "made of truth" (1)—and he says he believes her though he knows she is lying. She also tells him he is young, although both know he is not. As the speaker points out in sonnet 141, it is his "heart" that compels him to love her. His senses (eyes, ears, taste, smell) tell him otherwise, but his "foolish heart" cannot help serving her (10). In sonnet 149 the speaker laments his loss of self-respect. He claims that in his love for the Dark Lady he works "against" (2) his own interests. All of his "best" is spent worshiping her "defect" (11)—her weaknesses.

The speaker's judgment escapes him in his relationship with the Dark Lady. In sonnet 131 he knows she is as "tyrannous" as those "beauties" whom others admire, but he still admits to loving her. In his "judgment" her "black is fairest" (12), a statement that reads like a paradox: "black" and "fair" are opposites in reference to coloring. In sonnet 151 the speaker indicates that his passion defies his "conscience" (1). At the mere mention of his mistress's name, he finds his flesh "rising" (a sexual pun). The body has no conscience: in passion, it does what it will.

MOTIFS

Death is an important motif, or recurrent theme, in the sonnets. Shakespeare employs both vocabulary and imagery that relate to death and dying to emphasize his points, especially his commentary on the passing of time. At times Shakespeare capitalizes the D in death, personifying it with human actions and emotions to emphasize its force in life.

Many of these death motifs appear in the sonnets to the Fair Youth in which the speaker attempts to defy death and to immortalize his young friend in poetry. In sonnet 3 the speaker tells the Fair Youth that he can only maintain his beauty by marrying and having children before he dies: "Die single, and thine image dies with thee" (14). The speaker describes old age in sonnet 11 as "cold decay" (6), and Time argues with Decay for the right to age the Fair Youth in sonnet 15. In sonnet 18 the speaker tells his young friend: "Nor shall Death brag thou wand'rest in his shade / When in eternal lines to time thou grow'st." (11–12). Death will never be able to boast that the young friend has died and been forgotten, because the image of the Fair Youth will become a permanent part of time.

The speaker also focuses on his own death in a number of sonnets. In sonnet 32, for example, the speaker refers to death as "that churl" (2)—or rude person—who will eventually cover his bones "with dust" (2). In sonnet 64 he describes the thought that time will eventually take away his love as "a death" (13).

Shakespeare also employs many nature motifs in the sonnets. He uses seasonal images to compare the friend's youth to summer. In sonnet 5 the speaker warns the Fair Youth, "never-resting time leads summer on" (5)— his summertime youth will give way to autumnal middle age. The month of April appears in a number of sonnets as a metonymy for spring and nature's blooming. Flowers also appear in the sonnets: in sonnet 99 the speaker says that flowers have stolen their "sweet" fragrance and "color" (15) from the Fair Youth. In sonnet 94 the speaker states that summer flowers are "to the summer sweet" but die quickly if they become infected.

In sonnet 11 the speaker also reminds his young friend that "Nature" has chosen him not to perish but to multiply. The speaker tells the Fair Youth that "Nature's own hand painted" (1) a woman's face on him in sonnet 20. In sonnet 104 the speaker compares his young friend to the seasons that have passed in the three years they have known each other. He talks of "summers' pride" (4), "beauteous springs" (5), "April perfumes" (7), and "hot Junes" (7). This use of language conjures up images of the seasons.

Eyes are another image that recurs throughout the sonnet sequence. In sonnet 14 the speaker tells his friend that he reads the future in the young man's eyes: "from thine eyes my knowledge I derive" (9). In sonnet 24 the speaker compares his own eye to a painter that has portrayed his beloved's beauty in the "table" (2), or notebook, of his heart. Later in the same sonnet the speaker says that he sees himself reflected in his young lover's eyes. In sonnet 104 the speaker insists that this "fair friend" (1) will always look as he did when "first your eye I eyed" (2).

The speaker's eyes and heart wage a battle in sonnet 46. Both want complete control of the Fair Youth's image. At the end of the sonnet they agree that the eye owns the friend's "outward part" (13) and the heart possesses the "inward love" (14).

In the sonnets written to the Dark Lady, the speaker cannot seem to control what his eyes see. In sonnet 141 the speaker admits that his eyes see a "thousand errors" in his mistress, but his heart does not care (1–3). Sonnet 148 informs us that "Love" has put eyes in his head that "have no correspondence with true sight" (2). Therefore, the speaker calls his eyes "false" (5) and says that his tears are keeping him "blind" (13) to the truth about the Dark Lady.

SYMBOLS

Throughout literature, writers have often used the rose as a symbol of love and beauty. In the very first sonnet, Shakespeare mentions the flower and immediately defines it as "beauty's rose" (2). Therefore, the speaker establishes the rose as a symbol of his friend's youth and attractiveness.

In sonnet 35 the speaker appears to forgive the Fair Youth for something he has done. The speaker points out that "roses have thorns" (2) and that destructive worms often live in "sweetest bud" (4). With its thorns, the rose becomes a symbol of both the positive and negative sides of the Fair Youth's personality. The speaker also compares the Fair Youth's behavior to a rose in sonnet 95 and says that the young man's "shame" is "like a canker in the fragrant rose" (1–2). In sonnet 109 the speaker tells his young friend that he is his "all"—his everything—by referring to him as "my rose" (14).

The speaker describes beautiful roses that are "damasked" (5)—colored red and white—in sonnet 130. However, he describes the Dark Lady as having "no such roses" (6) in her cheeks.

The mirror—called a *glass* in Shakespeare's time—appears as a symbol in a number of sonnets. The mirror often functions as a symbol of truth, reflecting what the observer may not want to see. In sonnet 3 the speaker

SHAKESPEARE EXPLAINED: THE SONNETS

tells his young friend to look into his mirror and "tell the face thou viewest / Now is the time that face should form another" (1–2). The mirror reflects the truth about the inevitability of aging and the need to have children. In sonnet 77 the speaker tells his beloved friend that his "glass" (1) will show him how well his beauty will stand up to time. In line 5 he also claims that the young man's "glass" will, in time, reveal his "wrinkles." Shakespeare sometimes plays with this symbolism. In sonnet 22 the speaker insists that his "glass" will not "persuade" him that he is old as long as he is loved by the Fair Youth (1).

Shakespeare uses the color yellow as a symbol for aging and the passing of time in a number of sonnets. In sonnet 17 the speaker worries that his sonnets—referred to as his "papers"—might become "yellowed with their age" (9) and be discarded by the public. The speaker compares his aging state to autumn in sonnet 73 by describing "yellow leaves" (2) on trees. He repeats this symbol in sonnet 104 when he describes three beautiful springs turning into "yellow autumn" (5).

The color black—having nothing to do with race or ethnicity—often appears as a symbol of wickedness and impurity in the sonnets, especially those written to the dark mistress. In sonnet 131 the speaker admits that the Dark Lady's "black is fairest in my judgment's place" (12). The speaker refers to much more than her dark looks: her "black" symbolizes her negative behavior and seductive ways. As he says in the closing couplet, it is her "deeds" that are truly "black" (13), or foul and impure. He repeats this symbolic use of black in sonnet 147 when he tells the Dark Lady that she is "black as hell" (14), a reference to her sinful behavior.

LANGUAGE

The language of the sonnets is some of the most beautiful and clever Shakespeare ever composed. Modern readers must remember that the sonnet is a specific poetic form that follows certain rules. Shakespeare worked within these limits: he crafted fourteen-line poems, written in iambic pentameter (lines of ten syllables consisting of five alternating unstressed and stressed syllables called *iambs* and having a certain rhyme scheme). This demanding structure provides fertile ground for Shakespeare's heightened imagination and love of words.

Shakespeare fills his sonnets with rich imagery. Those images illustrate and reinforce the speaker's observations and feelings about life, love, fame, and aging. Sonnet 54 offers a fine example of Shakespeare's imagery-filled language, along with his argumentative style:

> O, how much more doth beauty beauteous seem
> By that sweet ornament which truth doth give!
> The rose looks fair, but fairer we it deem
> For that sweet odor which doth in it live.   4
> The canker blooms have full as deep a dye
> As the perfumèd tincture of the roses,
> Hang on such thorns, and play as wantonly,
> When summer's breath their maskèd buds discloses;   8
> But, for their virtue only is their show,
> They live unwooed, and unrespected fade,
> Die to themselves. Sweet roses do not so:
> Of their sweet deaths are sweetest odors made.   12
>   And so of you, beauteous and lovely youth,
>   When that shall vade, by verse distills your truth.

In this sonnet Shakespeare uses natural descriptions to make his point about the difference between flowers that have no scent and those that do. Whereas the "canker blooms"—another name for dog roses, or wild roses—have no fragrance, "sweet roses" do. As the sonnet progresses, Shakespeare cleverly crafts a contrast between beauty that is purely visual and beauty that is enhanced by fragrance. Still, careful readers will sense that this is not simply a sonnet about roses.

The speaker begins by referring to "beauty" and saying that it could be even more "beauteous" if it were also true. Truth, he argues, can "ornament," or decorate, beauty. By line 4 the "sweet odor" comes to represent truth. The Bard repeats the word "sweet" to unite the ornament of truth with the rose's fragrance. In these lines we see evidence of Shakespeare's rhetorical deftness with words. He has constructed a dichotomy, or division, of thought: beauty is good—but beauty *and* truth are better.

In Elizabethan times, readers would recognize "canker blooms" as a reference to wild roses. Like cultivated roses, wild roses also are red in color, but they lack the "perfumèd" aspect. The wild roses also have thorns and dance in the wind ("summer's breath"). Yet Shakespeare's use of the adverb "wantonly"—meaning "immorally" or "lewdly"—conjures up sexual connotations. For such a careful writer, it can be no accident that "wild" roses sway "wantonly" in the wind. Their petals are hidden in buds, but the wind reveals ("discloses") them. These loaded words convey a sexual undertone. The metaphor established early on has been extended throughout the sonnet.

Words dealing with behavior also surface in the third quatrain: "virtue" and "unrespected." Because the wild roses have only beauty for "show," they die "unwooed." The sonnet implies that no one will court (or woo) those who have only beauty and no truth. The contrast resurfaces in lines 11 to 12: cultivated roses with their sweet fragrance never die because their fragrance is turned into perfume. Therefore, the impossible happens: a flower that blooms and then dies manages to go on living as a perfume. The perfume is distilled from the essence of roses.

By shifting to second person in the closing couplet—directed at the Fair Youth—Shakespeare brings home the speaker's point. The youth may be "beauteous and lovely," but eventually those characteristics will fade ("vade," an archaic word no longer in use). Instead, the speaker's "verse" will distill the "truth" about the young man and—like the perfume—maintain his essence. Much repetition in both words and ideas occurs throughout the sonnets, connecting them both linguistically and thematically.

Sonnet 54 also offers a fine example of the poetic device known as a *conceit*. "Originally meaning a concept or image, 'conceit' came to be the term for figures of speech which establish a striking parallel—usually an elaborate parallel—between two very dissimilar things or situations." Throughout the sonnet, Shakespeare compares the fragrant rose to true beauty and the scentless wild rose to artificial beauty. As the sonnet proceeds, truth moves from being something added to beauty—an ornament—to part of its essence (like the sweet rose's fragrance).

INTERPRETING THE SONNETS

LITERARY EXERCISE OR CONFESSIONAL POEM?

What attracted Shakespeare to the sonnet form? Sonnets were extremely popular in Elizabethan England, and many of Shakespeare's contemporaries—such as Sir Philip Sidney—composed sonnets. Curiously, we cannot know for certain whether Shakespeare ever wanted his sonnets to be published. Still, four hundred years after they were written, they continue to captivate and challenge readers.

The sonnet imposes a specific format on the poet, but within that format it also offers a useful structure for expressing one's thoughts and feelings. In the Elizabethan, or Shakespearean, sonnet, each of the three quatrains provides a distinct space for developing ideas. Shakespeare skillfully connected the quatrains not only with rhyme but also by repeating ideas, words, and images. Shakespeare, like many sonnet composers, used the closing couplet either to sum up his thoughts or to offer an inventive turn of phrase or change in tone.

The Bard's sonnets also reinforce one of the format's greatest strengths: its form seems especially suited to the theme of love. The sonnet's specific and limited form forces poets to express their emotions within a very intellectual structure. In this sense, sonnets seem to represent a mental space allowing poets to organize their thoughts and feelings in a specific manner. For a highly imaginative and inventive lover of language such as Shakespeare, the sonnet form probably posed a welcome challenge to the Bard's abilities.

Shakespeare was also creative enough to change the typical topics of most sonnets and sonnet sequences. He rejected the standard use of a blond, idealized woman who is beyond the poet's reach. Instead, he replaced her with two unusual objects of affection: a younger man who has won the poet's affection and a mysterious woman with a shaky reputation and an even shakier moral character. Shakespeare then plays within his own invention by creating situations involving betrayal, lewd public behavior, competition from another poet, and a love triangle involving an affair between his two loves.

Over the centuries, many of the world's most respected poets have written sonnets. These poets include: Edmund Spenser, John Milton, John Keats, William Wordsworth, William Butler Yeats, Edna St. Vincent Millay, Robert Frost, e. e. cummings, Robert Lowell, and Pablo Neruda. Although the sonnet began as an art form, in modern times it has become more personal and confessional in nature. In America in the mid–twentieth century, Confessional Poets such as Robert Lowell and John Berryman composed a number of revealing sonnets. In 1947 Berryman produced an extremely personal sonnet sequence, *Sonnets to Chris* (published in 1967).

Because the speaker appears to address the first 126 sonnets to another man, scholars have often wrestled with the question of Shakespeare's sexuality. Over the centuries, some publishers have even changed the gender of the pronouns in the sonnets to the Fair Youth to make him a woman. Because we cannot know with certainty the identity of the Fair Youth—or if he even existed or refers to only one person—it becomes difficult to view the sonnets as autobiographical. More importantly, attitudes toward sexuality and friendship between two men were notably different in Shakespeare's time than they are in the twenty-first century. Still, we cannot deny the powerful emotions the speaker expresses in the sonnets written to the young man.

Modern readers must remember that no one in Shakespeare's time would have referred to him- or herself as "gay" or "homosexual": the latter word simply did not exist until the late nineteenth century. People surely had homosexual relationships but did not define themselves in those terms. The scholar Colin Burrow points out that "in early modern England male friends shared books, beds, and occasionally also women. . . . Men embraced and kissed each other with far greater freedom than most Anglo-Saxon males do now." Attitudes toward affection between two men—and the expression of it—were simply different.

More importantly, the sonnets to the Fair Youth offer various views of the speaker's relationship with him. At times the speaker seems completely enamored of the young man; at others he tells him to marry and have children. In some sonnets the speaker admonishes the Fair Youth for his public behavior, and in others the older speaker is jealous that another poet has shown interest in his young friend. Perhaps most tellingly, none of the sonnets clearly indicates the Fair Youth's feelings for the speaker.

Shakespeare scholar Stephen Booth has observed that "Shakespeare was almost certainly homosexual, bisexual, or heterosexual. The sonnets provide no evidence on the matter."

The sonnets to the Dark Lady are undeniably more sexual: they include more sexual puns and more direct references to sexuality. In comparison, the sonnets to the Fair Youth seem more spiritual and less bawdy. However, many scholars view this distinction as part of the attitudes toward women in Renaissance England. Although the speaker may have wanted a more intimate relationship with the Fair Youth, he cannot express his feelings in the same blunt terms he uses with his dark mistress. A number of scholars working in queer studies, a branch of scholarship dealing with sexual orientation and gender, have pointed out the more homoerotic aspects of the sonnets.

We know very little about Shakespeare's personal life other than the fact that he married and fathered three children. However, readers and scholars continue to speculate about the sexual preferences of the speaker in the sonnets.

READING THE DARK LADY

For centuries scholars have tried to determine not only the identity but also the ethnicity of the mysterious mistress of Shakespeare's sonnets. Some have tried to argue that the Dark Lady is "dark" only in her immoral behavior—although the speaker describes her as physically dark, especially in sonnet 130.

Whereas many sonneteers writing before Shakespeare created fair, blond objects of worship in their sonnet sequences, Shakespeare chose a woman with a dark complexion and black hair. Some scholars have taken the description of her hair as "black wires" in sonnet 130 to indicate that the Dark Lady may have been of African descent. Others have argued that she was not British but, perhaps, of Italian origin. In 1910 the English playwright

LOVERS SHARE A PASSIONATE KISS IN THIS NINETEENTH-CENTURY PAINTING, ENTITLED *THE KISS*, BY FRANCESCO HAYEZ.

George Bernard Shaw wrote a play entitled *The Dark Lady of the Sonnets*. In this fictional story of Shakespeare, Queen Elizabeth, and the Dark Lady, Shaw presents Mary Fitton as the real Dark Lady—even though he did not actually accept that explanation!

Some feminist critics point out that scholars tend to associate the negative with the Dark Lady and the positive with the Fair Youth, even though it is unclear whom the speaker is addressing in some of the sonnets because the subject's gender is left unspecified. The feminist critic Heather Dubrow has observed that "recognizing that some sonnets among the first 126 could refer to the Dark Lady implies much about that figure, the speaker, and the culture that contributed to constructing them." Some have seen class divisions in the two main figures of the sonnet: the speaker praises the Fair Youth who is of higher social status but insults the Dark Lady, whose social position is unclear.

The Dark Lady is one of Shakespeare's most complicated creations. The speaker seems to love her despite her faults in some sonnets. In others she represents a person of deceit and immorality. In some the speaker appears to accuse her of having a venereal disease. In his introduction in *The Oxford Shakespeare Complete Sonnets and Poems*, Colin Burrow claims that "her role is slightly different in each poem, and there is no particular reason to think of her as one person."

Chronology

1564 William Shakespeare is born on April 23 in Stratford-upon-Avon, England

1578–1582 Span of Shakespeare's "Lost Years," covering the time between leaving school and marrying Anne Hathaway of Stratford

1582 At age eighteen Shakespeare marries Anne Hathaway, age twenty-six, on November 28

1583 Susanna Shakespeare, William and Anne's first child, is born in May, six months after the wedding

1584 Birth of twins Hamnet and Judith Shakespeare

1585–1592 Shakespeare leaves his family in Stratford to become an actor and playwright in a London theater company

1587 Public beheading of Mary, Queen of Scots

1593–1594 The Bubonic (Black) Plague closes theaters in London

1594–1596 As a leading playwright, Shakespeare creates some of his most popular work, including *A Midsummer Night's Dream* and *Romeo and Juliet*

1596 Hamnet Shakespeare dies in August at age eleven, possibly of plague

1596–1597	*The Merchant of Venice* and *Henry IV, Part One*, most likely are written
1599	The Globe Theater opens
1600	*Julius Caesar* is first performed at the Globe
1600–1601	*Hamlet* is believed to have been written
1601–1602	*Twelfth Night* is probably composed
1603	Queen Elizabeth dies; Scottish king James VI succeeds her and becomes England's James I
1604	Shakespeare pens *Othello*
1605	*Macbeth* is composed
1608–1610	London's theaters are forced to close when the plague returns and kills an estimated 33,000 people
1611	*The Tempest* is written
1613	The Globe Theater is destroyed by fire
1614	Reopening of the Globe
1616	Shakespeare dies on April 23
1623	Anne Hathaway, Shakespeare's widow, dies; a collection of Shakespeare's plays, known as the First Folio, is published

Source Notes

p. 54, par. 3, "The word 'travel' . . .": Robert Matz, *Shakespeare's Sonnets*. www.shakespeares-sonnets.com.

p. 54, par. 4, *see* Colin Burrow, ed., *The Oxford Shakespeare Complete Sonnets and Poems*. (Oxford and New York: Oxford University Press, 2002) 434.

p. 60, par. 3, For more on Shakespeare's indebtedness to classical poets, *see* Burrow, ed., 490.

p. 65, par. 3, For more on the sound of the bell's toll, *see* Burrow, ed., 522.

p. 69, par. 3, Matz, www.shakespeares-sonnets.com.

p. 73, par. 3, For more on the sexual pun in sonnet 95, *see* Burrow, ed., 570.

p. 76, par. 1, "In sonnet 116 . . .": Robert Matz, *The World of Shakespeare's Sonnets* (Jefferson, NC: McFarland & Company, 2008) 96.

p. 76, par. 5–p. 77, par. 1, A *writ of error* definition can be found in Burrow, ed., 612.

p. 77, par. 2, "depict an illicit . . .": Alfred Harbage, ed., *William Shakespeare: The Complete Books* (Baltimore, MD: Penguin Books, 1969) 1451.

p. 80, par. 2, For more on meanings of the word *spirit*, *see* Burrow, ed., 638.

p. 80, par. 5, "presents us with two . . .": Helen Vendler, *The Art of Shakespeare's Sonnets* (Cambridge: Harvard University Press, 1997) 553.

p. 90, par. 3, "The paradox of the sonnet . . .": Vendler, 619.

p. 92, par. 3, "Shakespeare's young man . . .": Douglas Bush, "Shakespeare's Sonnets," in Harbage, ed., 1451.

p. 93, par. 1, The nondefining nature of sexual activity can be found in Burrow, ed., 125.

p. 108, par. 2, "Originally meaning a concept . . .": M. H. Abrams, *A Glossary of Literary Terms*, 6th ed. (Fort Worth, TX: Harcourt Brace Jovanovich, 1985) 32.

p. 110, par. 2, "in early modern England . . .": Burrow, ed., 126.

p. 111, par. 1, "Shakespeare was almost . . .": Stephen Booth, *Shakespeare's Sonnets* (Yale: Yale University Press, 1978) 548.

p. 112, par. 2, "recognizing that some sonnets . . .": Heather Dubrow, "'Incertainties now crown themselves assur'd'" in *Shakespeare's Sonnets. Critical Essays*, edited by James Schiffer (New York: Garland, 2000) 113–133.

p. 113, par. 3, "her role is slightly different. . . ," Burrow, ed., 131.

A Shakespeare Glossary

The student should not try to memorize these, but only refer to them as needed. We can never stress enough that the best way to learn Shakespeare's language is simply to *hear* it—to hear it spoken well by good actors. After all, small children master every language on Earth through their ears, without studying dictionaries, and we should master Shakespeare, as much as possible, the same way.

addition — a name or title (knight, duke, duchess, king, etc.)
admire — to marvel
affect — to like or love; to be attracted to
an — if ("An I tell you that, I'll be hanged.")
approve — to prove or confirm
attend — to pay attention
belike — probably
beseech — to beg or request
betimes — soon; early
bondman — a slave
bootless — futile; useless; in vain
broil — a battle
charge — expense, responsibility; to command or accuse
clepe, clept — to name; named
common — of the common people; below the nobility
conceit — imagination
condition — social rank; quality
countenance — face; appearance; favor
cousin — a relative
cry you mercy — beg your pardon
curious — careful; attentive to detail
dear — expensive
discourse — to converse; conversation
discover — to reveal or uncover
dispatch — to speed or hurry; to send; to kill
doubt — to suspect

entreat — to beg or appeal

envy — to hate or resent; hatred; resentment

ere — before

ever, e'er — always

eyne — eyes

fain — gladly

fare — to eat; to prosper

favor — face, privilege

fellow — a peer or equal

filial — of a child toward his or her parent

fine — an end; "in fine" = in sum

fond — foolish

fool — a darling

genius — a good or evil spirit

gentle — well-bred; not common

gentleman — one whose labor was done by servants (Note: to call someone a *gentleman* was not a mere compliment on his manners; it meant that he was above the common people.)

gentles — people of quality

get — to beget (a child)

go to — "go on"; "come off it"

go we — let us go

haply — perhaps

happily — by chance; fortunately

hard by — nearby

heavy — sad or serious

husbandry — thrift; economy

instant — immediate

kind — one's nature; species

knave — a villain; a poor man

lady — a woman of high social rank (Note: *lady* was not a synonym for *woman* or *polite woman*; it was not a compliment, but, like *gentleman*, simply a word referring to one's actual legal status in society.)

leave — permission; "take my leave" = depart (with permission)

lief, lieve — "I had as lief" = I would just as soon; I would rather

like — to please; "it likes me not" = it is disagreeable to me

livery — the uniform of a nobleman's servants; emblem
mark — notice; pay attention
morrow — morning
needs — necessarily
nice — too fussy or fastidious
owe — to own
passing — very
peculiar — individual; exclusive
privy — private; secret
proper — handsome; one's very own ("his proper son")
protest — to insist or declare
quite — completely
require — request
several — different; various
severally — separately
sirrah — a term used to address social inferiors
sooth — truth
state — condition; social rank
still — always; persistently
success — result(s)
surfeit — fullness
touching — concerning; about; as for
translate — to transform
unfold — to disclose
villain — a low or evil person; originally, a peasant
voice — a vote; consent; approval
vouchsafe — to confide or grant
vulgar — common
want — to lack
weeds — clothing
what ho — "hello, there!"
wherefore — why
wit — intelligence; sanity
withal — moreover; nevertheless
without — outside
would — wish

Suggested Essay Topics

1. Choose a sonnet and write a response to it from the point of view of the person Shakespeare is addressing. Respond specifically to the statements made by the speaker in the sonnet. It may be a sonnet of praise or of insult—but indicate in your essay that you have fully understood the poet's overall idea in this specific poem.

2. Discuss the role that social class plays in the sonnets. How does the social class of the speaker, the Fair Youth, and the Dark Lady come into play in the sonnets? Is the speaker affected by the class of the person to whom he is speaking? Is his language or attitude different? Offer examples from different sonnets to prove your point.

3. Argue for or against Shakespeare's commentary on aging in many of the sonnets. Do you agree that a person can only overcome aging and death by having children or by having someone write about him or her? Find some comments about aging in different sonnets and respond to them.

4. In a well-developed essay, consider the friendship between the poet and the Fair Youth and compare it to modern friendships between men. We live in very different times than Shakespeare, yet most people want and need friends. What would be the advantages and disadvantages of expressing feelings for one's friends so openly? Is there anything about friendship we can learn from the Elizabethan approach?

5. Defend the Dark Lady! Using examples from the sonnets addressed to the speaker's mysterious mistress, write a defense of the Dark Lady and her behavior. While we hear a great deal about her, we know very little about the speaker's own behavior in the relationship. Consider looking at the relationship from her point of view. Also, would the speaker be so critical of the Dark Lady in modern times?

Further Information

BOOKS

Bloom, Harold. *The Sonnets.* Bloom's Shakespeare through the Ages. New York: Chelsea House, 2008.

Matz, Robert. *The World of Shakespeare's Sonnets.* Jefferson, NC: McFarland & Company, 2008.

Mowat, Barbara A., and Paul Werstine, eds. *Shakespeare's Sonnets.* Folger Shakespeare Library. New York: Washington Square, 2004.

Shakespeare, William. *The Oxford Shakespeare: Complete Sonnets and Poems.* Edited by Colin Burrow. Oxford and New York: Oxford University Press, 2002.

Shakespeare, William. *The Sonnets.* The Pelican Shakespeare. Edited by Stephen Orgel. New York: Penguin Classics, 2001.

WEBSITES

www.playshakespeare.com
Play Shakespeare features the text of all the sonnets with an online glossary, reviews, a discussion forum, and links to festivals worldwide.

www.shakespeare-online.com
Shakespeare Online features analyses of the sonnets, along with translations into contemporary English, information on biography, plays, books, the theater, study topics, and videos about Shakespeare.

www.shakespeares-sonnets.com
Shakespeare's Sonnets includes the text of all the sonnets with detailed notes, explanations, illustrations, and cultural references.

Bibliography

Abrams, M. H. *A Glossary of Literary Terms*, 6th ed. Fort Worth, TX: Harcourt Brace Jovanovich, 1985.

Burrow, Colin. "Introduction." *The Oxford Shakespeare: Complete Sonnets and Poems*. Edited by Burrow. Oxford and New York: Oxford University Press, 2002, 1–158.

Bush, Douglas. "Shakespeare's Sonnets." *William Shakespeare: The Complete Works*. Edited by Alfred Harbage. Baltimore, MD: Penguin Books, 1969.

Hall, James. *Dictionary of Subjects & Symbols in Art*. Boulder, CO: Westview Press, 1979.

Matz, Robert. *The World of Shakespeare's Sonnets*. Jefferson, NC: McFarland & Company, 2008.

Schiffer, James, ed. *Shakespeare's Sonnets*. Critical Essays. New York: Garland, 2000.

Vendler, Helen. *The Art of Shakespeare's Sonnets*. Cambridge, MA: Harvard University Press, 1997.

Index

Page numbers in **boldface** are illustrations.

SHAKESPEARE EXPLAINED: THE SONNETS

Index

Page numbers in **boldface** are illustrations.

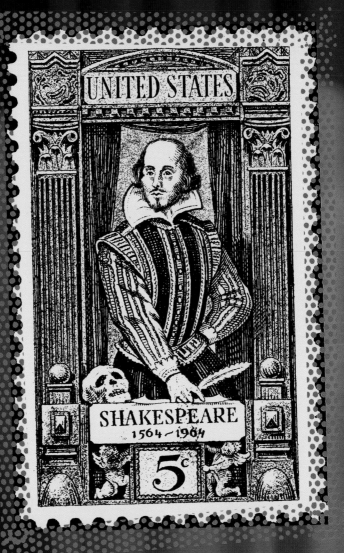

About the Author

Mark Mussari is a freelance writer and educator living in Tucson, Arizona. He has his Ph.D. in Scandinavian Languages and Literature from the University of Washington and taught for a number of years at Villanova University. He is the author of nonfiction books, academic journal articles, encyclopedia entries, and numerous magazine articles on art, design, and entertainment.